REV. FRANCIS R. DAVIS

You Shall Be Witnesses

You Shall Be Witnesses

Dennis J. Geaney, O.S.A.

FIDES PUBLISHERS, INC. ● NOTRE DAME, INDIANA

© Copyright: 1963, FIDES PUBLISHERS, INC.
Notre Dame, Indiana

Nihil Obstat: Reverend Francis P. Sullivan, O.S.A.,
Censor Librorum

Imprimi Potest: Very Reverend Francis J. Cavanaugh, O.S.A.,
Provincial

Imprimatur: ✠ Leo A. Pursley, D.D.
Bishop of Fort Wayne-South Bend

Library of Congress Catalog Card Number: 63-12045

By the same author:

You Are Not Your Own (FIDES, 1954)
Christians in a Changing World (FIDES, 1959)

Dedicated to

BILL and LAURA

and

JOE and MADELINE

CONTENTS

	Introduction	9
I.	God Loves Me	13
II.	Flesh for the Word	19
III.	To Find Oneself	27
IV.	The Layman Today	35
V.	Individualism Reviewed	43
VI.	The Layman's Cloister	49
VII.	"Things Are in the Saddle"	57
VIII.	The Worth of Work	63
IX.	The Positive Power of Penance	69
X.	Freedom to Love	77
XI.	The Meaning of the Mass	87
XII.	"Pray Without Ceasing"	97
XIII.	Mysticism in Action	107
XIV.	Forming the Catholic Conscience	119
XV.	Group Support	129
XVI.	Spiritual Counsel	137
	Conclusion—Peter of East St. Louis	145

INTRODUCTION

I arrived at the Smith home at nine-thirty on a Saturday morning. The logistics involved in getting there had been neatly worked out. It had to be on a day when I was in the general area and when the family was at home together. When I arrived, however, the wife and oldest daughter had left. The daughter was having her Saturday morning ballet lesson and it was her mother's turn to drive her to it. The husband, who worked evenings, was preparing his breakfast. The second oldest son entered to seek permission to be gone for the day. The ordinary parental inquiry involving names of companions, place, nature of activity, food, and time of arrival home took place. This was not a mechanical check list to get through so that the father could go on talking to a visitor. Rather, it was a genuine human, loving encounter of a father and ten-year-old son.

Our conversation was again interrupted by the return to the household of the oldest son who announced that he had to serve an eleven o'clock wedding Mass at the parish church three miles away, to which there was no public transportation. It was now ten-thirty. A crisis was averted when I volunteered to be the baby sitter for an infant and a three-year-old while the father taxied the son and his companion to church in a car that runs well with only three springs. I forgot about our anticipated high-level talk on lay spirituality when the responsibilities I had voluntarily assumed dawned upon me. Supposing the baby cried—or something worse happened? My anxiety subsided when I reflected on the wonders of the telephone and also the possibility of standing at the door and yelling to the neighbors for help. The baby did whimper. I felt I had to act with the decisiveness of a President in moments of international crisis. If there was not prompt action, a whimper could be a wail. I decided on using the three-year-old as a buffer. I lifted her into the playpen, risking the possibility of having two bawling babies instead of one. The strategy worked. I could now wait out in a more becoming manner the arrival of one of the parents.

It was time to prepare the noonday meal when the mother arrived. We discussed ways and means of buying meat in quantities at sales. When the dinner was served I thought it out of place to discuss lay spirituality. This would be the last time that day the children would be gathered together in this family setting with their father. He would soon be off to work. Before I departed the husband apologized for not having had time for the discussion we had been looking forward to for months. He added that if the morning's hectic family life was not to them a prayer, then for them there was no prayer.

Actually the trip was very worthwhile. It taught me an extremely important lesson. It is within this framework of car pools to be arranged, meals to be served, and crises to be faced that the Christian life of lay people is to be lived. Lay sanctity is to be forged from cars that won't start in the morning, from babies that cry to be fed and changed, from children that need the reassurance that comes from being listened to with love or lifted with loving arms, from the long trek back and forth to work, from the community meeting at which more meetings are planned. Sanctity for the layman can only be achieved from the broken pieces of an untidy day.

Our age is called the age of the laity. In the words of Romano Guardini, "The Church has come alive in the hearts of men." The call of the popes for lay apostolic action has evoked a desire for the degree of sanctity necessary to support such action. Lay people are showing a growing dissatisfaction with a diet of trimmings and frosting. They want to bite into the stuff of sanctity. In a college commencement address Cardinal Cushing summarized these latent lay desires for holiness:

> The evidence of recent history points to the sanctification of the laity as the major ferment going on in the world-wide Church. There is evidence at every hand: the surprising number of lay people who clearly desire a more than ordinary holy life, the increase of interest in religion among Catholics and non-Catholics alike, the number of devoted lay people who do not find their place in the religious life, and yet desire an intense Christianity. The evidence of the specialized Catholic Action movement is particularly impressive. They have held out the highest ideals of sanctity to their members and even have begun to produce contemplatives within the lay state.
> There is also the evidence of the ordinary Catholic layman, especially many young intellectuals. They may not yearn for martyrdom or mystical prayer. They may even long for a routine bourgeois life in the suburbs, with only conventional religious practices. But they are deeply committed to parish life and parish schools, and they are the strength of the new revivals of liturgy and discussion. Unless they are blind, they are beginning to see the handwriting on the wall: "It is no longer possible to be mediocre. Are you for Me or against Me?" They are open to the call to lay sanctity.

There is no ritual act for the layman who, after a dark night of mediocrity or groping for the light switch, discovers the riches of the Christian life. He does not change his name like a biblical figure, or a monk or nun. He does not change his residence or his type of work like a monk who goes off to a monastery. If he is married, he does not take the vow of celibacy. Discerning friends and intimates, however, can recognize that there has been a "conversion" or a breakthrough. He has come to grips with God's love for him. He wants to set out on the road to lay sanctity. He now seeks maps and guides to help him chart his way. No book can make his decisions for him. This book simply seeks to offer some suggestions to the beginner and encouragement to the seasoned traveler.

The author is indebted to the people who filled out a questionnaire which elicited free-floating thoughts and convictions about the modern American layman's struggle for sanctity in a bread-and-butter, beer-and-pretzel world. Added to this were countless conversations on this subject in scores of cities and towns across the country. In the beginning there was an attempt to count and codify these reactions. This cumbersome arrangement was set aside for the author's own synthesis of the layman's quest for God. He wishes also to express his indebtedness to those individuals and groups he found in his work as an itinerant preacher.

I

GOD LOVES ME

The mystery of mysteries is that God loves me. We have rattled off these words in singsong catechism responses. We have added our amens to prayers that were studded with pious phrases about God's love for us. At the same time we have carefully avoided any reflection on the words lest they disturb our cozy relations with God. If we let down our defenses and permit the words to penetrate to the core of our being, what we presently call peace will be disturbed.

This idea should not be considered lightly. There is risk involved. The thought that God loves me has the power literally to drive me to drink or to other forms of escape. It may disturb a person's peace to the point that, within the framework of his present commitments, he may approximate an answer to Christ's call "to sell what thou hast, give to the poor, and come follow Me." He may even begin to treat his enemies kindly. Once disturbed he can never go back. Love or guilt will rule his life.

We cannot comprehend God's love because we cannot comprehend God. This is not our immediate obstacle. The difficulty is more comprehensible, more earthly and concrete. It is not that He loves, but that He loves *me*. I can somehow grasp the notion that He loves in a vague way the whole human race, but for God to love *me*. . . . For God to love me in such a way

He would rather die than be without me, that He loves me in an unchangeable way is something I cannot grasp. It is difficult to believe that I am worth the death of anyone, least of all an all-holy God.

Our technological society reinforces our sense of unworthiness. No longer are jail inmates and servicemen the only ones designated by numbers. We are numbers to the Social Security office, to the telephone company, to the gasoline dealer and restaurant when we present our credit cards, to our parish through our Sunday envelopes. The branding iron of the rancher was simple compared to the extensive coding system which distinguishes the vital facts of our life by holes punched in IBM cards. In the financial centers of the country our lives are fed to monstrous machines which sort us and categorize us without the possibility of human error.

A number system which substitutes mechanical efficiency for untidy human relations can be an obstacle to our comprehension of God's personal love for each of us. When numbers replace warm and loving human relationships, there is no experience of human love. Without this loving encounter with my fellow man, I cannot love myself.

Love is a tricky word. In this book self-love will be used as the opposite of selfishness. Self-love is open and self-respecting; it means that I try to love or respect myself as God loves or respects me. Respect, according to its Latin origin, means "to look at." God looks at me and loves me. I must learn to look at myself and see in myself what God sees in me and finds so precious.

When self-love has dried up in the human heart, there is no possibility of experiencing divine love. The key to the mystery of God's love for me is buried in my power to love myself. My self-love or self-respect feeds upon my exchange of love with those I am related to in my daily rounds of worship, work, and play. Any diminution of these encounters makes God more remote and inaccessible.

The necessity and benefits of a coding system cannot be denied. With the multiplication of relationships among all the inhabitants of the world, the IBM machine becomes a symbol of world-wide impersonal relationships on a scale we could never have dreamed of a quarter of a century ago. The Christian response to this development must be positive. The impersonality of our giant structures must be countered by the effort to infuse new depths of love in existing relationships. Our present system must be made a conductor of human love and a foretaste of the divine embrace.

To treat people as things is an ever-present temptation. Recently, in leaving Chicago's Union Station my eyes gravitated to a newspaper headline. Maybe it was my concern for the people in the Congo which led me to buy the paper. With my eyes still on the paper I reached into my pocket, passed some coins to an outstretched hand and, without taking my eyes from the paper, picked it from the stand and continued toward the exit. Then, as I left the station, I reflected on what I had just done. In my eagerness to identify with the harassed Congolese, I affronted the dignity of the man selling the papers. By not giving him a "thank you" or an appreciative nod, I treated a fellow man like a vending machine. When a man is continually treated as a machine, his respect for himself must diminish. A shrivelled humanity has a shrunken capacity for receiving the rays of God's love.

The charm schools which are proliferating illustrate our tendency to use people as things. Charm becomes a marketable commodity rather than a spiritual quality. Girls want poise and pretty faces. Boys want to date girls with pretty faces. Mothers want daughters to have pretty faces because a daughter with a pretty face gives her mother acceptability in her circle of married friends. Fathers want daughters with pretty faces. The advertising media and TV personalities remind fathers that a daughter with a pretty face is a precious prestige symbol. This can all add up to tragedy for the person behind that pretty face. Long before the face wrinkles she may wonder why she is not loved for her own sake, instead of simply being admired and sought for her decorative effects. Without an experience of true love which is neither admiring, manipulating, moralizing, nor reforming, she may equate looks with love. How can the girl with the pretty face who is loved by her parents for her looks and treated by boy friends as a thing instead of a person believe she is loved by God?

When others fail to respect us for our likeness to God, we lose the I-Thou relationship with our fellow man. In an impersonal world the "I" becomes an "it." To Dun and Bradstreet, a person is a $500 risk; to the nurse, a coronary in 602; to the mailman, 802 Fourth Street; to the waitress, a good tip; to the clothing salesman, a medium size; to the boss, an efficient worker; to a mother, a child who cleans his plate; to a white man, a Negro who knows his place; to the Negro, Boss; to a husband, a wife who can really cook; to a wife, a husband who is a good provider; to a party boss, a straight ticket; to a TV pitchman, a detergent buyer. Despite the role-playing demanded by our complex and highly specialized society, I must always remain an "I." The other must be a "Thou," and God my Lover and the source of human love.

The neighborhood grocery store was once a means of human solidarity. As the butcher cut the meat to suit the eating habits of each family, he listened to and exchanged bits of local gossip. He tied the community together to the same degree that the supermarket has destroyed it. The price we pay in the fragmentation of the neighborhood community can be seen as a woman moves her cart through the aisles. It is no place for neighborly chitchat that relieves the tensions of the housewife. The color combinations which are the result of motivational-research studies speak in place of the fatherly figure of the grocer of her childhood. The check-out girl cannot look at her customer while she glances at the packages and nimbly records the prices on her machine.

This loss must be compensated for in other aspects of life if the community of mankind is to hold together. Unless the saved time, the improved diet, and the lowered costs provided by the supermarket are used to create new and meaningful human relations, then the supermarket has been a step backward in our efforts to come to terms with God's love for us.

One Thanksgiving Day I joined an American family who had invited thirty foreign students and visitors to their home for the traditional American Thanksgiving ritual. Prior to the era of frozen foods, prepared mixes, paper plates, and the facility of shopping in supermarkets, such a meal could not be served without a staff of hired help and days of preparation. Now, through the efficiency of the supermarket, the alchemy of this family's world-embracing love can make their home a neighborhood United Nations and anteroom for the Kingdom of God and His reign of love.

With us, human and divine love are always intertwined. The Christian grows in the love of God as his responses become more human, as he practices the art of loving and becomes more lovable. If Christianity means becoming more human through the practice of love, it is strange that even Christians should fear achieving a love relationship with God through loving His human images.

Instead of desiring to refine his sensitivity so as to become more responsive to his neighbor's feelings, the typical Anglo-American Catholic prefers to find his contact with God in a code of do's and don'ts. He places his security in an adding-machine approach to heaven. He finds religious satisfaction in clicking off rosaries, chalking up indulgences, setting records for reception of the sacraments, Masses attended, and fasts kept. Making the means become ends, he prefers the posturings of a ritualism divorced from his loves and hates, his joys and anguishes, his fears and follies, to a life of charity.

The comfortable Christian wants to be left alone with his sentimental and comfortable Christianity. He does not want God to draw too near in human garb. He understands too well Christ's words to Angela of Foligno: "It is no laughing matter that I have loved you." Love of God spelled out in human terms may cause violence to erupt in us. God is love and the response that this jealous Lover demands will always be a scandal and a stumbling block.

The saint is as shocked at God's love and its implacable demands upon his ego and convenience as is the satisfied parishioner who wants no new, disturbing demands on his life. A saint who grasped the implication of God's love for him said: "Lord, are you mad to wish me well?" To Paul, Christ's love for us was the height of foolishness. He called it "the folly of the Cross." "Foolishness" has always been used to describe the love relationship. The question posed in terms of foolishness is: "Should I be fool enough to love Him who was fool enough to become involved with a fool like me?" If the response is affirmative, we owe our friends a warning. They will be shocked to see us in our new roles as disturbers of the Christian's "peaceful" lethargy.

II

FLESH FOR THE WORD

A priest friend once told me of saying Mass at one of the shrines in the land of our Lord's birth. He was annoyed by the confusion of other priests saying Mass close to him, by the dirt, untidyness, and noise about him. He wished that he could be in some remote place where he would be removed from the distraction and confusion of the people about him. Then it occurred to him what the Incarnation or birth of Christ really means. Christ did not come to a neat and tidy world. Rather He inserted himself into the messy, sordid affairs of men. He did not run away from the sight and stench of evil. He could only heal the world by accepting all of it with a warm and loving embrace. My friend continued with Mass no longer finding distraction in external confusion. It became part of the world he was offering and consecrating to God through the Mass.

The Incarnation must be at the root of a spirituality for lay people. Spirit and flesh must be joined in the human person who seeks union with God. The tendency to separate these realities is often detected in people who view religion and religious practices as soul-saving devices. Have you ever met a soul? Thus far I have met only persons. Their spiritual aspirations and emotional blocks are reflected in their eyes, their voices, their mannerisms, in the entire complex of their emotional responses and actions.

At the same time that I am a priest I am a man, and can only communicate with others as a man, that is, through my feelings, words, and actions. In life, body and soul can be separated only intellectually. The real separation will begin at death. We deny our humanity and the Incarnation when we anticipate death by treating each other as disincarnate spirits. How dull and lifeless would our relationships with one another be if we treated each other in soul-to-soul fashion! How disastrous to a marriage for a wife to demand her husband to treat her only as a soul!

There has always been a schizophrenic tendency among Christians. People always want to put aside the ugly and the real and pretend it does not exist. In the name of seeking holiness, they seek a spiritual life divorced from the dregs and refuse which accumulate from our daily dealings with one another.

A spirituality for lay people cannot be rooted in alienation, rejection, or repression of what offends our sensitivities. It is based on facing up to both the hardness and shallowness in ourselves that recoils and escapes from the sight of sufferings. Growth in the love of God must be pivoted on the Incarnation. This means a loving acceptance of our human qualities, both good and bad, and our relationships with our fellow men with whom we are joined by the common humanity which we share with them and Christ.

God so loved the world that He willed to identify Himself forever with the human race. He did not want to be removed from mankind as a creator is from his creation. This identification came from His fleshing out of the Word. On March 25 we celebrate the Feast of the Annunciation of the Blessed Virgin, which was once called the Feast of the Conception of Christ. On this day we commemorate the eternal Son of God clothing Himself in our flesh. At the moment Mary said, "Be it done unto me . . . ," He vested Himself with our humanity. This we call the Incarnation. It is the linking of the human and divine natures, or God and man, in the person of Christ.

We cannot ponder the mystery of God's enfleshment too much. Can the world be such a bad place if Christ identified Himself with it by walking its streets and roads, sleeping under its skies, and eating the food from its fields?

When we sin through our senses, we may wish we were pure spirits and were not weighed down by the promptings to sin we find in our bodies. In these black moments it is reassuring to know that Christ used these senses to touch, taste, see, smell, and hear all the wonders of the natural world and the world of his fellow men. He was sensitive to the simple wonders of nature—the fields ready for the harvest, the seasons with their changes. He likewise sensed what was sordid. His nostrils caught the stench of drains and the perfume of harlots. His emotions were refined to the degree that He was often moved by compassion at the sight of suffering. He wept at the death of Lazarus. He gave vent to His anger when He called the Pharisees "a brood of vipers."

Too often we think of our senses and emotions only as potential enemies that might embarrass and betray us. In moments of depression from lapses in purity, one may fail to appreciate the gift of sex and not realize that the sexless person is a defective person. The person without feelings cannot share in the sufferings of his fellow man. The Incarnation tells us that our passions can be instruments of love. Only through the control and refinement of our humanity can compassion break through and summon us to raise our voices against injustice and to give comfort to the afflicted.

Christ did not view mankind with lofty disdain from a pinnacle of sanctity. He became embroiled in human encounters. He was violently angry at the injustice and double talk of the Pharisees. With the money-changers at the temple He acted out His anger. Prostitutes and blind beggars won His loving attention and understanding. He had the skill of a diplomat or defense attorney before His accusers and the abandon of a starry-eyed reformer when He pleaded that we should do good to those who hate and persecute us.

An acceptance of the implications of the Incarnation makes us kin through our common humanity with the unwed mother, the illegitimate child, the mongoloid baby, the alcoholic, the straying husband, the delinquent juvenile, the nation that takes our dollars and accuses us of imperialism, the white Catholic who protests a Negro move-in, the Negro who is filled with bitterness, the idle rich who have contempt for the shiftless poor, the ungrateful poor who bite the loving hand that feeds them, the ulcer-ridden status seeker, and with all of us who are unable to see our own moral weakness or are too proud to align ourselves with other moral weaklings like ourselves. We can root ourselves in Christ only after we have pledged allegiance to our humanity with all its perverse inclinations. We can transcend our wounded humanity only by embracing it. This truth is symbolized for us in the Cross. To accept the incarnational view of the Christian life means to embrace suffering in ourselves and others. It means the gradual death of all our selfishness, which amounts to nothing less than a life of white martyrdom.

Christ is linked to us by His sharing of our human nature. We are linked to Him by sharing His divine nature. It was an unequal exchange in which God permitted Himself to be robbed and man to be enriched. God traded a share in His divine nature for a stake in ours. We brought Him down to a level with misfits and weaklings like ourselves. He gave us a share in the life of the Trinity and companionship with saints and angels. This share in the divine life comes to us with our induction into the Mystical Body. Baptism brings us membership in God's holy people—people not made holy by their moral perfections but by God's prodigious gift of Himself.

Why did our Lord weep over Jerusalem? He wept because He loved it. Could we weep over New York, Chicago, or any city we call our own? Undoubtedly there are reasons for tears, but we do not find ourselves as committed to our city as our Lord was to His. We can easily understand Christ weeping over the death of Lazarus, but to weep over a social body, a political and religious institution, seems beyond comprehension.

The answer lies hidden in the mystery of the Incarnation. Our Lord did more than vest Himself with a body with senses and emotions. His humanity found its expression in a person with a network of social ties. Every person belongs to a particular family, neighborhood, occupational group, parish, city, country, and civilization. These providential circumstances are the cause and the result of our mutual dependence. They imply a giving and a receiving without which we cannot live humanly. They demand commitments, and commitments demand loyalties.

Our Lord did not appear among us as a world citizen such as the Secretary General of the United Nations. He was localized by every political, cultural, and religious dimension of His day. He belonged to a particular century, a particular people, to a religion with its own ritual, to a family with a certain genealogy. He spoke with the accent of His clan. Everything about Him—beard, voice, clothes—identified Him as a man committed to the destinies of the people with whom He cast His lot as a man.

Our Lord did not simply tolerate the customs and traditions of His times. He embraced His culture, His civilization. He listened to its tunes. He prayed its prayers. He enjoyed its wedding feasts. The history and traditions of His people were woven into the fabric of His life. The thought of the loss of all this, symbolized in the destruction of the Temple, shook him visibly, to the point of tears.

An incarnational spirituality seems at times to create more problems than it solves. The smallest child at play in the neighborhood knows that it cannot do whatever it wants. This is an elementary lesson in child training. The high-school student who wants to incarnate herself in teen life is warned by her elders at home, school, and church and by her favorite "Dear Ann" columnist that lines must be drawn and barricades erected at the danger zones. The adult is told that there is a Christian family, business, and civic ethic that sets limits beyond which he must not trespass.

How can we identify with those around us who live by codes foreign to ours? Is not isolation a better way to preserve a code of values than the risky business of jeopardizing all in our eagerness to be at one with our peers? Is it wise to encourage lay Catholics brought up in a ghetto tradition to place in danger their precious heritage for uncertain gain?

Such questions no longer have any validity. Ghetto living in a pluralistic society is an anomaly. It is unfeasible and unrealistic. Whatever the dangers may be for Catholics who get into the mainstream of American life, there is no alternative to facing them. Our only choice is to identify with our surroundings in a way that is completely human and Catholic. We must embrace all that conforms and reject all that conflicts with Christ's gospel of love.

Since we live in the most dynamic culture in the history of mankind, the rules for a past generation cease to fit the next. The principles remain, but the circumstances are in an endless process of change. Books are written about problems which have been solved. Lectures and sermons are given about situations which are as dated as the piracy of the Robber Barons and the inhumanity of slave trading. Lay people at every moment are pressed to make decisions in their unique circumstances. They must learn to be satisfied with clues and insights rather than foolproof answers. New challenges will meet them when they move from school to work, from one phase of work to another, from single to married life. Living by a conscience developed in the fourth grade or by rules learned by rote in Catholic high schools and colleges puts the Christian at a serious disadvantage. He is unable to adapt himself and be a tower of strength to those who are tossed about by conflicting opinions and practices.

There is no substitute for a dialogue among Christians faced with similar circumstances in life. Christian values on the grassroots level of society are best formed by people who with open Bibles in their hands attempt through discussion to form a collective judgment on a common problem. At best they can only approximate what Christ would have done under similar circumstances. An incarnational view of life never gives us the certainty of the rigid moralist whose answers are categorical, coded, and of universal application. To pivot one's life on the Incarnation will make us willingly settle for conclusions that are tentative, untidy, and always in the process of evolving. While it disturbs the rigid, it offers an exciting challenge to the flexible and warmly human. It is the only approach which can keep Christianity viable in a changing world.

III

TO FIND ONESELF

With married adults the subject of choosing a vocation is a matter for their youngsters to explore. The couple has chosen marriage. The husband has a job which he may or may not like. Ordinarily there is little possibility or desirability of taking up another line of work. A twenty-year mortgage, the hardships involved in changing cities, neighborhoods, companies, homes, and schools are reasons which ordinarily rule against risking the uncertainties of a new economic venture. For most men in their forties the door on their occupational or professional life is as tightly locked as the door on their married life.

The mistake one could make in reading the above paragraph is to equate occupational life and marriage with vocation in such a way as to assume that the choice of these states of life closes off further discussion or development of the notion of vocation. A husband's job and a wife's household work are only part of the stuff from which a vocation is discovered and lived. Into the mixture should go all of our time and talents, not merely those needed in the strict line of duty. It is from the totality of our waking day with its struggles, hopes, and commitments that a vocation is gradually formed and ultimately solidly fashioned. This concept of vocation is dynamic rather than static. It is something that is always emerging and unfolding until our last breath, when we begin our enduring vocation of enjoying the endless wonders of God's beauty.

The man who, although conditioned to the monotony of work, seeing his job simply as a means of supporting his family and affording him free time to devote to politics, his Church, or TV, fails to see his work as a providential calling. The fact that he can be as easily replaced as a part of the machine at which he works may preclude his ever having this heightened sense of vocation. The lack of the possibility of creativity in his work may force him to seek creative expressions in other areas of his life. The housewife who has little patience with housework, preparing meals, wiping noses, telling stories, listening to lessons, has no sense of vocation as a mother.

The St. Vincent de Paul Society or Legion of Mary member who visits a poor family, brings medicine to the sick, or shows friendship to a person who has strayed away from the Faith, ordinarily has a refined sense of vocation about this kind of work. He may say to himself: "This is meaningful to me. It is something in which I am uniquely competent. This is what God wants from me. There are nights when I would prefer to stay home or spend an evening with the boys, but I manage to shake off my lethargy and get out on my rounds. I would say that I am well satisfied with my choice, even though I was not fully aware of what was involved when I was asked to join."

The housewife who sets up an easel in the basement and picks up her brushes and paints in an odd hour when the children are napping, even if she has to postpone her washing and mending, may find in this solitary hour what vocation means. In this spare hour she comes to grips with the core of her being and expresses her deepest feelings. She should have no puritanical guilt-feelings about the pleasure attending this creative work (which may never get out of the basement). Instead of thinking of all the undone good in the community, she might consider how much more of herself she can give to her community and family because of this restorative activity.

The housewife who brings order into her family commitments to the point that she can without scruple devote some time to a community organization, and a husband who spends a few evenings a month as a part-time politician serving on a local government committee, may reach an awareness that through these aspects of their lives they are finding self-fulfillment as human beings and citizens. In discovering their roles as citizens they are putting another piece of the vocation puzzle in place.

I once heard a state legislator say that there were conceivably other people in his district who could replace him as representative, but no one else could be father to his children. This meant, not that he wanted to give up political office, but that he was conscious of the tension or conflict that resulted from his dual roles of legislator and father. At this juncture in his life both were included in his total Christian vocation.

Vocation implies either an initial positive choice or the loving acceptance of what had been previously accepted with reluctance. It is an awareness of the creative possibilities of a situation and the positive desire to identify oneself with it. It is the growing realization that *I* can do this job, that there is a relationship between my abilities and this task. It is a decision to accept these providential circumstances, to embrace them as Christ embraced the Cross, carrying the load with external agony and inner peace.

Usually the decision is a process of growth which may not be marked by a single conscious experience of having made a choice. There may be moments of insight when the reality of the struggle to make a choice is seen clearly. Ordinarily any dramatic decision that marks plainly a turn in our life is the culmination of years of minor decisions and little insights gleaned from experience. All of these pile up, waiting for the moment of truth or decision when the one called solemnly declares to himself that this is his work, his vocation, his niche in life, that this is the area in life in which he is going to make his contribution to the world.

We do not wait for a vocation to come to us. We assess the present, look to the future, and make a decision. The religious vocational literature emphasizes the call as coming from God. But God does not speak in one manner to people called to a priestly or religious vocation and in another to people called to a lay vocation. He speaks to all through their talents and their opportunities.

A vocation is always in the process of growth. As the years go on it becomes clearer in its details. I have not been using the word in the sense of a general calling to a certain state or occupation. I am talking about the very particular meaning our lives have in our unique circumstances. I am discussing vocation in the way I discussed God's love. We are not chosen in groups or loved as identical beings coming from the same mold. Every person is called to play a definite part in the drama of redemption. This part is unique in the sense that I alone can play it. It is not something, like a hat, that I can wear or not wear. It is a part of my being because I have accepted the responsibility for it.

"Vocation" as used in this chapter is what the psychologist refers to as identity. It is precisely what distinguishes us from others, first of all in our own minds. This is a positive self-image. It is not the false image of what we might have been or might become but the complete acceptance of the reality of what we are, with all the human and apostolic opportunities and responsibilities inherent in our situations.

An emotional attraction to a particular type of work may mislead us as to our vocation. Emotions are blind and never substitutes for reason. A vocation can be a heavy burden. Graham Greene's priest in *The Power and the Glory* was a man weighed down by his vocation. He rebelled against it and at the same time understood his call and suffered the shame and agony that came both from the vocation and from his human weakness.

James Baldwin, a young American Negro writer expresses this feeling of being burdened with a vocation. He writes of himself: "I am a writer; that sounds grandiloquent, but the truth is that I don't think that, seriously speaking, anybody in his right mind would want to be a writer. But you do discover that you are a writer and then you haven't any choice. You live that life or you don't live any." He is obviously writing of himself when he says: "All artists, if they are to survive, are forced, at last, to tell the whole story, to vomit the anguish up."

There is always the feeling of inadequacy. Can I ever live up to this calling, be it that of plumber or politician, truck driver or Trappist? After the decision is made scruples are set aside. We must accept our own limitations. God picks frail people to do His work. This is the history of vocations in the Bible. When God spoke to Jeremias and told him he had chosen him to be "a prophet unto the nations," Jeremias thought only of his inadequacy. "And I said: 'Ah, ah, ah, Lord God! Behold, I cannot speak, for I am a child.' And the Lord said to me: 'Say not, I am a child: for thou shalt go to all that I send thee: and whatsoever I shall command thee, thou shalt speak. Be not afraid of their presence: for I am with thee to deliver thee. . . .'"

Vocation in the sense of establishing an identity means finding one's opportunities, the useful things which he can do for others and which justify him as a person who makes a distinctive contribution to the community. To find one's vocation is to find oneself. Our Lord tells us that if we wish to find ourselves, we must lose ourselves. While the life and death of someone like Dr. Tom Dooley can dramatize this loss of the excess baggage of selfish desires and the discovery of our creative and outgoing selves, everyone can find his true vocation or real identity in his present circumstances.

The terminal cancer patient can learn with the eagerness of a child that suffering can be creative and redemptive, that it can pump new life into the arteries of the Mystical Body. The sit-in in the Jackson, Mississippi, jail can discover his identity through witnessing to the truth as John the Baptist did in Herod's jail by daring to speak up and be counted down. It is difficult to be enthusiastic about routine chores, but for most people vocation must be seen in terms of the undramatic—the dishes and diapers, the unending monotony of never-changing chores. Vocation means leaving the world of childish immaturity with its toys and selfish satisfactions and looking with new vision at the people around us and discovering the obvious needs, such as friendship, which we can satisfy.

In an interview after his election, President Kennedy said: "Sure it's a big job. But I don't know anybody who can do it better than I can...." Does this sound like the voice of pride speaking, or like Isaias after his lips have been cleansed by fire: "And I heard the voice of the Lord saying: Whom shall I send? And who shall go for us? And I said, 'Lo, here am I, send me'" (Isaias 6:8). Throughout the campaign which ended in Kennedy's election, the American electorate were at times bewildered by two relatively young men stumping the country with unabashed confidence in themselves, repeating tirelessly to millions of people the words of Isaias, "Send me." Strangely there was little obvious envy of Kennedy and Nixon. Most people make no secret of their longing to be the common man. Possibly our Lord had this secret longing as he knelt in the Garden of Olives. He had to pay the price for His singularity, for setting Himself up as the champion of the oppressed.

Those who write about youth make the same indictment of them as those who describe the man in the gray flannel suit. Neither category of people want to expose themselves to the risk of failure. They prefer cushioned comforts to the possibility of ridicule for failure. They prefer the protective shell of mediocrity. Humility becomes confused with timidity. They are interested in trips to the moon—by other people. For themselves, they are satisfied to watch with cool detachment from their TV chairs.

Only once have I heard a person proclaim himself to be a modern prophet. He was a priest speaking to priests about the apostolate to the Spanish-speaking Catholics of North America. With the intensity of an Old Testament prophet he spoke of a special vocation within the broader calling to the priesthood. The next day I tried to copy down from memory his message. "I decide," he said, "what is the will of God for me. This job has to be done. I am not specifically assigned to it, but I see what has to be done. I will wait no longer for special approval or a command from higher authorities. I will take my mandate from the circumstances of this stinking social evil and declare myself a prophet, as one anointed with the natural intelligence, courage, and ability to do the job."

This is the language of all the great founders of religious orders and reformers in the Church. It is the language of the great artist, whether he be a poet, statesman, or a janitor with a sense of the dignity of his work. With mystic vision he sees reality in all its untidy dimensions and humbly puts himself at the service of this most demanding master, cruel reality.

The modern prophet, cleric or layman, needs the humility to bare his soul to the world and risk failure and ridicule. Risk or challenge is the language of lovers. Only the daring need apply. The world is waiting for lay prophets to accept responsibility for restoring the world to Christ. In accepting this responsibility they will discover their vocation.

IV

THE LAYMAN TODAY

Why are we disturbed by people standing all day in the rain or cold selling *The Watchtower?* Why do visits to our homes by Jehovah's Witnesses upset us? It might be that the Witness is stirring up guilt feelings about our relationship to our Church. Maybe they are rebuking us for our failure to stand all day Saturday outside a downtown department store with copies of *America* or *The Sign* in our hands while we receive the snubs of respectable shoppers. Maybe they suggest the bitter truth that we buy our way out of service in our Church with our Sunday envelope offering. Maybe somewhere in our subconscious the devoted pentecostal worker is nagging us about our refusal to give a night a week to one of the many parish or diocesan organizations which supply some local, regional, or city-wide need.

The American Catholic layman has been called the sleeping giant. With all the calls by popes, bishops, pastors, with the examples of acute needs flung in his face, he has hardly blinked an eye. In spite of all the books, pamphlets, and admonitions from the pulpit he is not quite sure that there is a genuine place for him. It may be that he believes with our Protestant brethren that the Catholic Church is hierarchically dominated and there is little place for the layman's unique talents, intelligence, and opinions. The layman's seeming apathy or reluctance may not be due entirely to his lack of generosity but also in part to his encounters with the Church on the local scene. He may show great insight in feeling that he is not trusted in his parish, when he sees the money being counted and banked every week by consecrated hands.

The structure of the early Church was a proliferation of local communities which were more like large families than efficiently run organizations. The social distinctions between clergy and laity were not as pronounced as they are today. It was the community which had the errand or mission which we call the apostolate of the Church. All were apostles, but each was to witness according to his gifts or role in the community.

The essence of the errand or message is that Jesus Christ, Son of God, by His death and resurrection wills to save, through the Church, all who believe in His name. The apostolate in the early Church centered around the celebration of the liturgy and the serving of the poor, widows, and orphans. In the era of martyrdom the liturgy prepared the Christians for the lions. St. Ignatius of Antioch was eager for the encounter: "I am the wheat of Christ; may I be ground by the teeth of beasts that I may be found pure bread." There was a notable absence of philosophizing, theorizing, and organizational procedures. There was spirit and life but little form.

All witness must be based on sincerity. Christian witness stands or falls by its unswerving attachment to the virtues of our Lord. The pure Gospel spirit can be stifled by techniques, programs, and blueprints. We always need a St. Francis of Assisi to remind us of the practicality of the Sermon on the Mount. In our age the Little Brothers of Jesus, following the spiritual writings of Charles de Foucauld, have for their sole purpose witness to the poverty and charity of Jesus. They teach no classes, seek no converts, administer no sacraments, have no special apostolate to the poor or sick. They simply live among the poor, support themselves with the labor of their hands, and pray in an abode which is no different from the others in the area. They exist to witness to Christ's life by their presence.

The Little Brothers also exist to be witnesses for simplicity and integrity to all of us who are involved in the complex organizational structures of our day. The living presence of Christ must go out from us as the rays do from the sun. Any specialized apostolate or occupation in which we engage must reflect in its unique way an evangelical simplicity and genuine love. To plead for simplicity is not to parrot the line of the anti-organization, anti-intellectual simplist. Probably the most quoted lines from Pope John's *Mater et Magistra* are those which deal with the very real complexity which faces the modern man:

> Socialization is, at one and the same time, an effect and a cause of the growing intervention of the state in areas which, since they touch the deepest concerns of the human person, are not without considerable importance nor devoid of danger. Among these are care of health, instruction and education of the young, control of professional careers, methods of care and rehabilitation of those physically or mentally handicapped in any way. Socialization, however, is also the fruit and expression of a natural tendency almost irrepressible in human beings— the tendency to unite for the purpose of obtaining objectives which each ambitions but which are beyond the capacity of individuals.
>
> This sort of tendency has given rise, especially in these latter decades, to a wide range of groups, associations and institutions having economic, cultural, social, athletic, recreational, professional and political ends. They operate within a single nation and on a world-wide basis. It is clear that many benefits and advantages flow from socialization thus understood. (¶ 60-61.)

This tendency toward specialization reflects itself in the proliferation of organizations which the Catholic encounters on the diocesan and parish levels. In the field of marriage and pre-marriage education we have a wide range of movements and services. For parents with children in Catholic schools, there are auxiliary organizations which call upon parents for many forms of support. The inability to provide classrooms and teachers for all Catholic youth in our Catholic school system has expanded our catechetical program with volunteer lay teachers as the base.

Each parish has its peculiar needs and ways of dealing with them organizationally. Compiling a list of the variety of youth, special-interest, or service groups would be an endless chore and only prove the obvious. There is, however, a wide gap between the group that exists to perpetuate itself for the petty prestige of its officers and the groups that, while aware both of their limitations and of the felt needs of the people who constitute the group, are trying to serve real needs. Within the same diocese and parish there is rivalry for members. The core families hold multiple memberships in the parish organizations, while for the overwhelming majority the only tie with the Church is Sunday Mass.

The Church began to experience specialization shortly after the era of the Twelve Apostles. Contact with the pagan academic world was a threat to the looseness of our Lord's scattered utterances, which were often couched in the form of parables. At the risk of losing the evangelical simplicity of the Gospel narratives, scientific precision had to be given to words and statements. Christianity was forced to buttress the simplicity of our Lord's teachings with philosophical and theological systems.

The proclamation of the Gospel can no longer be done as simply as it was by Sts. Peter and Paul in the first century. Professional teaching standards and techniques are used in presenting the message to both the tiniest child and students in the international schools of theology. From two or three Christians gathered together informally to serve their brethren, we have developed organizations with trained public-relations staffs. To answer the call for lay assistance within the framework of our vast assortment of national, diocesan, and parish organizations, the lay Catholic must make almost as many choices as at a smorgasbord.

The above is only one side of the coin of lay responsibility. It is the church-orientated side. If the layman reads carefully the papal documents on the social teaching of the Church and the literature on Catholic Action, he will come to the conclusion that his occupational and community or political life also demand Christian witness. This, too, involves a further proliferation of organizations which vie for the services of community-minded people. The layman has never been confronted with a greater array of difficult choices.

There are some distinctions which must be made in putting the layman's role in perspective. The priest's apostolate or field of action will be *primarily* in the sacral order, that is, the realm of sacramental rites and pastoral duties. The layman's field will be primarily in the secular or temporal order, that is, the economic, political, and familial areas of life. The priest is essentially the mediator between God and the people; the layman is basically the mediator between the Church and the world. These distinctions are far from neat. The layman at times assists the priest in his priestly work, such as giving instructions in the faith. The priest may find himself in roles which are considered lay roles in our society, such as college administrator, or professor of economics or physics. It is pointless to press for precise divisions of labor.

Because we are living in an industrial, technical society in which lay life is autonomous and respected, the layman has a greater stake and influence in the affairs of men than he had in previous times. This is why Pius XII, in addressing lay people at a ceremony creating cardinals, said: "You are the front ranks of the Church." The work of the apostolate is the work of the whole Church. The work of the apostolate, then, is the general vocation of every confirmed layman, as presiding over the Mass is the general vocation of the ordained priest. The details of apostolic commitment can only be spelled out in terms of the talents, opportunities, and insights of the individual layman.

The Catholic layman is gradually distinguishing between that aspect of the apostolate which is the primary responsibility of the hierarchical Church and in which he is vitally needed to assist as a layman, and the lay apostolate, which is his because he is an executive, a mechanic, a scholar, or a father of a family. In the latter roles he must assume primary responsibility.

The hierarchical Church can only assist the layman with its social action documents, its study clubs, and its Catholic Action organizations which deal with temporal affairs as they touch the layman's responsibility for Christian action. It can be seen that the lay apostolate is not a design to ease the burden of the bishop or pastor, but an effort wherein the bishops and pastors help the layman to come to grips with tasks which are his and from which he cannot escape responsibility.

Before a new President enters the White House, he searches the universities, the financial, business, and labor centers of the country for the most talented people to carry out or administer his program. By American political standards, our Lord's search nineteen hundred years ago for a group of men to whom He would confide the building of His Church after His Ascension brought forth at best a second-rate team. They were severely limited in education, intelligence, and moral perfection. From a human viewpoint and without the insight of divine wisdom, they were glaringly inadequate for the task. Any appeal to the laity to assume responsibility for the mission of the Church should begin with God's own answer to the layman's plea of incompetency, inadequacy, and moral weakness.

When Samuel came to Bethlehem to find a successor to King Saul, the Lord said to Samuel, "Look not at his countenance, not on the height of his stature . . . nor do I judge according to the look of a man; for man seeth those things that appear, but the Lord beholdeth the heart." When Jesse brought his seven sons before Samuel, Samuel asked: "Are here all thy sons?" He replied, "There remaineth yet a young one who keeps the sheep." He was told to send for the youngster. David, the ruddy-faced lad, was brought to Samuel and anointed. Later David committed the sins of murder and adultery. Yet in spite of his sins God said of him that he was a man after His own heart.

Father John M. Fahey, S.J., in an issue of *Work* (March, 1961), wrote this for lay people in the field of social action:

If at times the job to be done almost overwhelms you, it is consoling to remember that in all history there has been no man who did not have many defects. Some didn't know enough; some, like Hamlet, too much. Some were too weak, some too strong; some were too changeable, some too conservative or unbending; some were too silent, some too loquacious; some were too ready to take advice, some were not ready enough; some were too cautious, some too rash; some were too arrogant, some too meek. Yet these men did achieve greatness, in spite of their defects.

If only the perfectly fit, intellectually and morally, were allowed to assume positions of responsibility, the world's work and the social apostolate, and even the Church, would soon come to an end. So, the social apostle must accept humbly the knowledge that he will be only fifty or sixty percent efficient in the tasks he has to do. But his inefficiency need not worry him. No matter what may be your intelligence, your experience or your education, you will find that they are not enough to overcome all the difficulties the active social apostle meets. Why worry?

When lay people plead incompetence to the call of the lay apostolate, our Lord confounds and confronts them with His choice of apostles. Incompetence can be replaced with competence if there is a willingness to submit to the discipline required to achieve it. The plea of moral weakness is only a subterfuge to escape responsibility. The weak can gradually become strong if they submit to God's overpowering grace. The common characteristic of prophets and apostles, ancient and modern, is a willingness to do one's best no matter what the cost, even if the cost be martyrdom.

V

INDIVIDUALISM REVIEWED

Once when I had to serve as a substitute pastor, among my duties was a convert instruction class. We had a lesson on the Eucharist, and in preparation I read the two chapters in the catechism on the subject. To my surprise my own basic approach to the Eucharist was not mentioned. This intrigued me. I looked around for another catechism to find if the catechism I first read was unusual. The second catechism did not differ.

I think of the Eucharist as the sacrament of brotherhood, or in St. Augustine's phrase, "O sign of unity, O bond of charity." Or in the sentence of St. Paul, "We being many are one Bread, one Body." Or in the liturgy of Corpus Christi, "O Lord, graciously bestow upon your Church the gifts of unity and peace which are symbolized in this sacrifice we offer you." Am I hypercritical of our catechisms, which have served our American Catholics since the Council of Baltimore in 1884 when I expect them to reflect this aspect of the Eucharist which is the flowering of Scripture, liturgy, and the teachings of the Fathers?

What did I find in the two catechisms in the rectory office? In the first catechism, which had thirty-two questions and answers, there was no reference to the Eucharist as a bond among men. In the second, six reasons were listed why our

Lord instituted the Eucharist. There was no hint there that union with our fellow man was a major reason. The catechisms are still fighting the battles of the sixteenth century, proving that Christ is really present under the Eucharistic species of bread and wine. In the questions on preparation for Holy Communion there is much about fasting and nothing about forgiveness of our brethren as a preparation for banqueting with members of Christ's Body. Nowhere could I find an approximation of Pius XII's explanation of the purpose of the reception of the Eucharist: "Holy Communion unites us to *each other* and to the Divine Head [of the Mystical Body]."

I found a different attitude toward the Eucharist in reading in a Protestant weekly of the results of the 1961 New Delhi meeting of the World Council of Churches. The writer went to great lengths to explain the scandal of the Lord's Table. Instead of there being only one table, there are many tables. This could be shocking only to one who believes that the Eucharist is a sign of unity. Protestants are indeed shocked at their own division at the Lord's Table simply because they believe in an almost forgotten Catholic truth: the Eucharist is the sacrament of brotherhood.

American Catholics have been raised on a concept of the Eucharist as a spiritual muscle builder. Everyone is out for himself as he makes his way to the altar rail. He is storing up graces against a nebulous enemy. He has been taught since childhood a strictly "Jesus and me" approach to Communion. He is not making his way to a family table but to an ecclesiastical automat. The result is that, after Communion, we think of the Eucharist as Christ really present in the bronze tabernacle rather than as Christ living through His Eucharistic action in the myriad and intricate human relationships in the community.

If the Eucharist is understood in terms of brotherhood or oneness in the Mystical Body, Christ becomes a dynamic force in the reshaping of the institutions of society. The Eucharist and charity are two sides of one coin—a dynamic, corporate Christianity. The old dies hard. The legacy of individualism will continue to remain with us. The crust of custom is not easily broken.

The public image of the Church reflects the results of our individualistic approach to the Eucharist and charity. At the grass-roots level, the Church appears to have little concern for disarmament, racial integration, or the concerns of Pope John as voiced in *Mater et Magistra*. On the contrary the Church appears interested in negative concerns which when examined in the context of real life have little relevance to world problems. In the legislative halls we appear as a vested-interest group when bills for federal aid to education exclude parochial school aid. It is not the stand itself on this issue which creates the image as much as the stand when placed against the background of our less than passionate concern with other humanitarian legislative endeavors in which we have no organizational stake. Legislatively we appear to be interested only in protecting our organizational status quo.

This negative image is further projected when our moralisms touch on matters of purity and aesthetics. Although our antismut and Marylike dress campaigns may be directed against a false view of sex, our lack of attention to other areas and our failure to emphasize positive aesthetic values give us the dour faces of Puritans. The total image we project is not that of a people who have given flesh to the authoritative papal documents on social questions, but that of defenders of the narrow concerns of a parochial, provincial, and puritanical Church. This is the type of parochialism which seems to have little concern for the masses of people whom Christ came to redeem, unless they prove themselves to be white, Anglo-Saxon, respectable, churchgoing, conforming Catholics. This is an attitude more Calvinistic than Catholic.

If we understood the Eucharist as fellowship in the Lord or as community worship, rather than as a form of individual piety unrelated to membership in the human race, we could more easily see the role of Christianity in shaping the institutions of society. Unless we choose the cloister or have a special vocation like that of a Little Brother of Jesus, who witnesses solely by his presence, it is nonsense for us to define charity or love exclusively in terms of good example. To love *in deed and in truth,* means to love in the most effective way we can in a complex and specialized society. It means bringing our charity to bear by working to change the economic, political, and familial institutions of society.

Cardinal Suhard put it this way: "Take careful note of this. The salvation of persons cannot be accomplished without a certain 'salvation' of the social order. . . . A priest will fail in his vocation if he confines his efforts to the salvation of persons, for he has not only souls for parishioners but problems, organizations and a given section of space and time in the city of this world."

If we are inclined to write this off as distinctively French, listen to the popes. Pope Pius XI wrote: "The personal apostolate can no longer suffice, if indeed it can be so much as maintained that it ever did suffice." Pope John XXIII writes: "From instruction and education one must pass to action. This is a task that belongs particularly to our sons, the laity, since their work generally involves them in temporal activities and *in the formation of institutions dealing with such affairs.*" (Emphasis added.)

American Catholics do show an interest in establishing a stable family life. The Church stands firm against divorce and artificial family limitation. It makes heroic sacrifices for its parochial schools. It promotes family Communions, family holy hours, family picnics, pre-Cana and Cana conferences and family retreats. Sermons identify the family as the basic unit of society; if we would work exclusively to save the family, it is urged, we would save society.

The family is indeed the basic biological and psychological unit in society, but, practically speaking, in the affairs of the world it is not basic. Do we hear of the family having a lobby in Washington and our state capitols as do farm, business, labor, education, and Church groups? Who speaks for the family? The family is the most fragile institution in society, the victim of every other institution. If the family is to strengthen itself, it must become concerned with changing the other institutions of society which prey upon it.

There is a school of thought among Catholic Action family groups which says that a family movement has no business mixing in politics and economic affairs. Senator Eugene McCarthy answers this objection: "It is not sufficient to humanize and sanctify the institution of the family alone. The family will not survive in a vacuum. Unless it exists in a community which is both human and Christian, it will be unable to fulfill its function as it should."

This human and Christian community necessary for integral family life will not come about until married people, wives as well as husbands, see their responsibility to all facets of the social order. It is true that a family movement cannot change economic and political institutions in the same way as do members of boards of directors and elected representatives of government, but each member of the movement brings his stone to the building of the common edifice by an active and enlightened awareness and by actions consonant with his status in life.

Thus far we have said two things in this chapter: first, we do not relate the Eucharist and love in our teaching; second, we do not see Christian love in its institutional ramifications. If, as our Lord affirms, love for one another is the badge of discipleship and if, as the popes affirm, this love must be put in terms of institutional actions and commitments, then we need a new formula for an examination of conscience.

James L. Cockrell, Jr., a Tulsa businessman, writes: "I have discussed spiritual development with many laymen and women. In almost every case, their concept of spiritual acts is Church-centered, or related to devotions of a more or less formal nature. Acts of charity are conceived as Christmas baskets, visits to the county poor farm, to hospitals, sometimes visits to prisoners.

"It is hard for them to see that a well-done job of work, a Community Chest board meeting, a friendly visit to a neighbor, is essentially a spiritual act; that a soft word to an irate spouse or child, providing clean clothes and nourishing food for the family, serving a community as a clerk in a utility company, or writing a letter to a Congressman favoring aid to underdeveloped nations is an act of real supernatural charity, often a heroic one."

Where do we learn that there are other categories of sins to confess besides anger, impurity, and beating one's spouse? Who formulates for us the proposition that choosing a Western TV show consistently over local civic meetings may be sinful? When do we hear that we might be committing a venial sin by choosing consistently the sports section of the newspaper to the exclusion of the parts dealing with domestic and international issues? There is no question about the need to update our examination of conscience on *the* Christian virtue, charity, which claims a primacy.

Cardinal Montini pleaded with the delegates to the Second World Lay Apostolic Congress to make the following resolution and program their own:

> We will love our brothers, whether they be close or distant. We will love our own fatherland, and we will love other fatherlands. We will love our friends, and we will love our enemies. We will love Catholics, and we will love schismatics, Protestants, Anglicans, the indifferent, Moslems, pagans, atheists.
> We will love all social classes, but particularly those which have most need of help, of assistance, of betterment. We will love the very young and the very old, the poor and the sick.
> We will love those who mock us, who despise us, who stand in our way, who persecute us. We will love those who are worthy of love, and those who are unworthy. We will love those who fight against us: we do not want any man to be our enemy. We will love our times, our community, our technical skills, our art, our sport, our world.
> We will love, and we will try to understand, to have compassion, to think well of others, to serve them, to bear with them. We will love with the heart of Christ: "Come to me, all you. . . ." We will love with God's good measure: "God so loved the world. . . ."

VI

THE LAYMAN'S CLOISTER

Our Lord's description of the Last Judgment is a dramatic literary piece. He enumerates six situations in which people of His day suffered need: hunger, thirst, homelessness, sickness, nakedness, and loneliness. Those who respond to these needs enter the kingdom of heaven; those who deny their neighbor these elementary services are cast into hell-fire with the devil and his angels. From the right with astonishment and from the left with anguish the same question is asked: "When did we see Thee in these conditions?" The answer, for weal or woe, is that Christ identifies Himself with the needy whoever, wherever, or in whatever conditions they may be.

Where there is a human need that I can fulfill, there is Christ as surely as I find Him in the Eucharist or will find Him in heaven. If my life is an unending response to human needs, I am joined with Him in continuous communion. The city streets, the noise of children, the discord of neighbors, the impertinent intruder, the late TV newscast cry for my understanding and assistance and thus bespeak Christ's presence to me.

The world becomes my cloister. The rhythm of its groans and man's response are the plain song of the earthly choirs of men who recognize the true identity of the needy. The whole world is my parish because of my responsibility to it through the universal brotherhood of human suffering. In this way can my heart beat with the Sacred Heart of Christ. The Sacred Heart is no longer merely a statue or a picture, a devotion or a prayer, but a way of life. The boundaries of the Sacred Heart's love are the universe. Can mine be less?

Our Lord's world was simple. News traveled by word of mouth. People traveled by foot or animal. Schools were an almost unknown luxury. Small-scale fishing and farming were the basis of the primitive economy. Unions, employers' associations, migrant workers' camps were unknown. Politics was simply paying taxes to the oppressor. The tools of war were less destructive than the weapons of a teen-age city gang engaged in a rumble. Space was nothing more than the air one breathed.

When national political candidates face the TV camera or crisscross the nation on a speaking tour, they are exposed to more people than existed on the face of the earth in our Lord's entire life. Our Lord used simple family and pastoral images to form the background for His teaching. For effectiveness He had no other option. The sum of knowledge and the gamut of human problems for the people with whom He dealt—in contrast with the population of our TV, space, UN, IQ era of specialization and complexity—could be summarized in a grade-school reader.

In spite of the uncluttered lives of the people whom He taught, His lessons on justice, love, and redemption have universal application. Our Lord could only make the applications against the background of the people to whom He spoke. He left it to His successors to apply the Gospel to their own situations. In a dynamic society this becomes an endless task. As new situations arise, new applications must be spelled out. During the past seventy years, from Leo XIII to John XXIII, Christ's vicars have poured out a steady stream of papal documents covering a wide range of social problems.

Who are the hungry today? They are the undernourished children in the vast pockets of poverty in our affluent society. Numerically they are the more than half the world's population who pull their bedcovers each night over half-full stomachs. How can we feed them? There is no simple answer.

Pope John in *Mater et Magistra* points to the complexity of the solution: "To insure a pattern of economic development that preserves a harmonious balance among all the sectors of production, government authorities must formulate a prudent agricultural policy. Such a public policy should cover questions of taxation, credit, social insurance, price protection, the fostering of processing industries and the adjustment of farm managerial structures."

Who are the thirsty? They are the people in countries which need technical help to desalinize the water. They are the people who suffer from droughts because of the lack of capital and scientific assistance needed to build vast irrigation dams. Pope John, an authentic interpreter of the Judgment scene, encourages this type of assistance: "With such aims in view, world and regional organizations, individual states, foundations and private societies today are offering such countries generous help and greater technical cooperation in all spheres of production. They are assisting thousands of young people to study in the universities of more advanced countries and to acquire an up-to-date scientific and professional formation. Meanwhile world banking institutions, single states and private persons often furnish capital and thus make possible the rise of a network of economic enterprises in the underdeveloped nations."

Who are the homeless? In many of the world's capitals refugees are still to be found. Over 100,000 Cubans have crossed over to Florida since the Castro take-over. Statistics never tell the story of families separated, the difficulties with a foreign culture and language, unemployment, slum housing, inadequate diet, the red tape of bureaucracy, the resentment and discrimination by natives. The Mexican bracero and the Texas Mexicans, as they follow the crops north in the spring, reap a "harvest of shame" for themselves and for our national dignity.

There is no single, simple way to deal with the refugee or the migrant. On the political level lawmakers must pass legislation which enables local communities to come to grips realistically with society's unwashed and unwanted, by providing adequate public services for these fellow members of the human race. Social agencies, private and public, must offer their professional services. Individuals on a voluntary basis must provide homes, gainful employment, and neighborly services. Even more elementary is the giving of understanding and acceptance to the stranger.

Who are the naked? The research chemist who discovers a process for making clothing from synthetic fibers may well hear the call of the Lord on the Last Day: "I was naked and you found a way of clothing cheaply the near naked in the underdeveloped countries."

The foreign student who may be well fed, housed, and clothed may find himself stripped of friendships because of his new life in an alien culture. The lonely person has been stripped naked of warm loving friendships. There are hundreds of thousands of foreign students and visitors in our country and our local communities every year who long to meet Americans and Christians in a more intimate setting than an academic or factory atmosphere. Among Catholic groups in the United States the Christian Family Movement and the National Council of Catholic Women have outstanding programs for offering hospitality to foreign students.

The naïve who think that good example is all that is necessary for Christian witness have no comprehension of the visits, letter writing, and telephone calls involved in the simple arrangement for a small group of students to have dinner with an American family on Christmas. After we have accepted the responsibility for offering hospitality to foreign students we may then be able to talk about Christmas dinners in our homes for the willing skid row derelicts and the American Negroes in the center of our cities who have never known what it is to sit in a living room at ease with a white family.

Who are the sick? In this country there is a sizable section of our senior citizens whose savings and social security benefits are not adequate to provide for their medical care. When we take an interest in promoting private and public insurance plans which assist the medically indigent, we are binding the wounds of hundreds of thousands of people who have spent the most productive years of their lives raising families and turning the wheels of industry for everyone's benefit.

The medical research students who spend their lives in developing antibiotics can expect to hear our Lord say: "I was sick in Africa and you through your long hours in the research laboratories extended human life for millions of people who would have died before reaching middle age." To the Dr. Schweitzers and Dr. Dooleys the glad welcome can be anticipated, "Come, you blessed of my Father, you trained local doctors and nurses for Me in Africa and Southeast Asia to carry on after you died."

Who are the prisoners? Many prisoners in our jails anticipate their release only to find that the bitter stigma of the "ex-con" drives them back to the only group which will give them acceptance, the loosely structured federation of unreformed criminals. Several years ago John and Mary Jones, a mature married couple, listened to a lecture on the "ex-con" by a renowned "Hoodlum Priest." Because of a decade of orientation to the Christian life which they had received through involvement in apostolic groups, their reaction was different from the response of the typical audience of contented Catholics. Instead of leaving the lecture with the satisfied feeling that "Father is doing a great job for those poor unfortunates," they asked themselves what they as responsible lay people could do about a situation with which they had no previous awareness. Their inquiry led them to one of the country's largest jails where they were able to discuss at first hand with the wardens and inmates the problems of readjustment to civilian life. They permitted their feelings to be assaulted by reality. The anxieties of the prisoners became their own. They were already involved.

The husband with his experience as a business executive and the wife with her background in community organization assessed the situation. On leaving jail the ex-convict had no employer or employee committee to welcome him to the factory or office. There was no ceremony which would approximate the return of the prodigal son. Worse, there were no jobs for people with the stigma of a jail record. Suspicion of the ex-convict leads to continual rejection of him, and this rejection becomes the road back to the brotherhood of the underground world of crime.

John and Mary knew that when something is the concern of everyone it is the concern of no one. They had to step into the breach. Experience had taught them the depth of Pius XI's dictum that "good example is not enough." Kind words and kind thoughts were not enough. Jobs had to be found. This could only be done by convincing employers of their Christian responsibility. To deal with the problem effectively, a working committee of employers, personnel experts and other skilled people had to be formed. The Citizens Committee for Employment was formed—in anticipation, one might say, of the Judgment at the Second Coming of the Lord.

The response of the Joneses to the needs of prisoners, while a modern application of the Judgment scene, is not a challenge that many encounter in their daily round of work and play. But what moved John and Mary to see that this was *their* responsibility? Undoubtedly it was their long history in facing challenges more obvious and closer to home. As they developed as Christians, their frontiers extended. Because the example of helping ex-convicts find jobs is so extraordinary, it helps illustrate what can happen to all Christians once they are keenly attuned to the needs of others and acquire some competency and confidence in themselves through simpler projects undertaken with love.

To determine one's own life within the framework of responsible government is a human right, the denial of which is a form of political slavery. The millions of people behind iron and bamboo curtains are the world's prisoners awaiting release by the court of world opinion. The Communist scourge acts as a prod to the Christian to use his own political freedoms with responsibility to aid in exposing the menace of Communism. The Birch-type group is the neurotic response of frightened people to a real enemy. The irrational fears of these guilt-ridden people drive them into a form of psychological slavery. In this bondage their emotions are so crippled that they suspect and fear all forms of government and neighborhood groups whose patterns of social thought differ from their own. The genuine hardheaded anti-Communist is emotionally secure, justified in his rational fears of the enemy, and positive in his efforts to root out the social injustices which breed Communism everywhere.

World peace, which requires disarmament or international control of nuclear weapons, can only be realistically achieved through world-wide political structures. At present the United Nations represents our admittedly feeble but only viable effort in that direction. Is it a legitimate expectation to hear Christ say: "I was a political captive in Communist China and your support of the United Nations as a world institution was a stand in behalf of my freedom"?

This interpretation of the Judgment scene is a far cry from the "Jesus and I" concept of religion which has been fed to us through our childhood catechism and religion classes. For an adult to break away from childhood with its narrow concept of neighbor and to examine his conscience in terms of universal brotherhood requires no less an effort than putting a kite-flying child into outer space.

VII

"THINGS ARE IN THE SADDLE..."

His relation to the amount, quality, and use of material things needed in family and work life will always be a point of conflict to the lay Christian with an incarnational view of life. Our Lord was both attached to and detached from things. He had no disdain or contempt for material things. He was alive to beauty. He rhapsodized about the lilies of the field. Yet He possessed nothing. He was born in one man's stable and died in another man's tomb and in between He had "no place whereupon to lay His head." He used things to support Him while on His Father's errand. It requires the balance of a tightrope walker to be attached to all the genuine values of our society without letting them hold sway over one's life.

Things have their own way of dominating our lives. If I am given a shiny object to place in my room, I can ignore it only so long. Someday a layer of dust on it will become apparent. A visitor in my absence may write with his finger in the dust, "Dust me." The piece of wood or metal now, like a child, cries out for attention.

The man with his portfolio of securities may claim he is as detached as his coupons are detachable. Very likely his political and economic philosophy, even his political party affiliation and businessman's club membership, will reveal that he is more deeply influenced by his desire to maintain the present market value of the portfolio than he is by any concern for the world's poor. On the other hand, the marginal worker without a securities portfolio may be inclined toward a Marxist philosophy because he lacks the opportunity to accumulate wealth. The poor can be dominated by the things they desire but do not possess.

We see excessive attachment to creatures in the possessive mother. She impedes the child's emotional growth by her smothering solicitude and shows her own moral weakness through this overly dependent relationship. The father who neglects his family for work or play evades responsibility for developing the normal emotional dependence of the family upon him.

Monastic or religious life has always exercised authority over the individual's use of things. The regulation by another of the use of property can keep a person from losing perspective with regard to his real needs. The religious life is not extreme in its deprivation of its members. In fact, the vow of poverty is just as much a vow of material security; it provides as well as it limits. The vow was not extreme enough for Charles de Foucauld, who left a Trappist monastery for the Holy Land to imitate in his own rigorous way the real poverty of our Lord. And the vow was not extreme enough for St. Benedict Labre, who left the monastery and became a beggar on the streets of Rome.

Emerson wrote almost a century ago that "things are in the saddle and ride mankind." In the last quarter century "things" have multiplied in such proportions that the typical American Catholic has made a prodigious economic advance. This multiplication and availability of material goods, coupled with increased opportunities for social advancement, demand unprecedented restraint from men in their use of things. Restraint for the layman can be more difficult than renunciation for the monk. Affluence must be a docile servant, not a bitch-goddess.

How does one achieve objectivity with regard to his own material needs and his responsibility to share his own accumulation of things with the needs of people everywhere? There is no rule of thumb that can be given to lay people. Each person must assess his own situation in life and make a provisional decision. He will always be revising his estimate of his needs and never be satisfied that he is meeting his responsibilities to himself, his family, and the community. This nagging unrest about these decisions is part of the price a layman pays for permitting himself to take the apostolate and the Incarnation seriously. There are, however, some basic attitudes about things which can serve as landmarks in making decisions.

The traditional Catholic attitude toward property has been colored by the concept of stewardship. Mankind has found out from experience that private ownership is the best legal arrangement for the holding and use of property. Behind the legal right to possession is divine ownership. God has given things to man to care for. He cannot use property as he pleases without regard for the needs of his fellow man. He is a steward for the Divine Master. Because he has a legal right to dispose of property in a certain way, it does not follow that he always has the moral right to do this.

Basically property belongs to the human race. Each by industry or inheritance acquires the right to administer a share of it. Each has a right only to what he needs. This is the traditional teaching on property by the Fathers of the Church. St. Augustine sums it up: "The superfluities of the rich are the necessities of the poor. Those who possess superfluities possess the goods of others." Catholic moral theology has always defended the right of the poor man, in an emergency, to take without guilt from an unwilling owner what is needed to sustain the poor man in life.

Who can say what he needs? Many of our needs are psychic. The middle-aged man who prides himself on his youthful appearance "needs" a larger car, a more exclusive neighborhood and a country club to compensate for his physical and psychic losses. The man who has achieved status as a judge and prominence in other civic roles can drive to the courthouse in a clunker. His judicial robes are a sufficient status symbol. He can use his jalopy as a form of rebellion against the necessary conformity in the rest of his life, as a display of ostentatious simplicity, or to compensate for a restricted childhood devoid of the normal playthings of that period.

Our vocation is our most realistic determinant of our needs. When we see the providential circumstances of our life as our vocation, then it is easy to see that there are certain material prerequisites necessary to carry that vocation out. A student needs a quiet place to study. A doctor needs an office. A carpenter needs a kit of tools. A large family needs many bedrooms. A married couple who use their home as a meeting place for discussion groups and meetings needs a large living room.

Work, income, transportation, school, location of family and friends will be determining factors in selecting the site of one's home. The make, year, styling, and number of cars in the family are decisions which will revolve around income, work, availability of other transportation facilities. While the psychic need for status symbols and the common practice of one's peer group are to be reckoned with, each of us must set his own standards.

Each person and each family establishes a hierarchy of values. Modern advertising will try to upset our patterns by pandering to our irrational fears and latent anxieties. We may succumb and permit social pressure from our neighbors, relatives, and friends to exercise a tyranny over us that is more restricting than life in a concentration camp. Values will conflict; choices will have to be made.

Seldom will it be as easy as choosing between a new car or a new baby. However, what price range of clothes, what cut of meat to buy, whether to take a vacation at home or away, are decisions that daily cry out for conscientious answers. The choices become easier and somewhat routine the more clearly a person or family establishes its vocation, or unique apostolate. Growth in emotional security through the acceptance of long-range and other-worldly goals also minimizes our dependence on things and make decisions less agonizing. All material things are to be seen in terms of their service of God.

How can a Christian live by middle- or upper-income American economic standards when people in the same city are living on a lower than subsistence diet and without adequate medical care? Or how can one eat from a table overladen with food when there are millions of people in the emerging nations of the world bursting with new life but without the material resources to support it? I can remember vividly a wife in the presence of myself and her husband giving reasons why they should give up upper middle-income living standards and move to the slums. I knew that I had been cast in a role in which I was expected to argue against her pleadings and appease her guilt feelings. I did. There was no evident reason why this family should take up residence in the slums. Their middle-class background had not prepared them for an apostolate among the people of such an area. These people would not accept them unless they completely stripped themselves of their former tastes, conveniences, and habits of life. This cannot be done easily or without extraordinary motivation.

Such a move would mean that the couple would be giving up the opportunity to make a real testimony to Christian poverty in a status-conscious middle-class suburban area—a fruitful apostolate, but one without the romantic attraction that comes from leaving the comfortable surroundings of one's childhood and adult life.

Are there some limits to the amount of material goods one can acquire and use for one's own comfort? Can a Christian under any conditions justify a quarter-of-a-million-dollar coming-out party for his debutante daughter? Without denying the need of social life for young people, or the need for the rite of initiation into adult life which only comes once in life and which even tribal life recognized as having genuine social value, the display of such an event must be a scandal of Christianity to the non-Christians in Africa and a vulgar display of opulence to those Christians, wherever they are, who are living on the thin edge of economic endurance. Those of us who do not have the money for such displays can vent our spleen over them, but we still have the responsibility of setting limits to the use of what we do have.

Most Americans confronted by the grinding and involuntary poverty of others are like the stranger who, while riding through the slums of an Asian city, wished he were enveloped by a London fog. Facing the reality of almost universal world poverty can only be a disturbing experience. We can establish rapport with our suffering brethren all over the world by our interest in the politics, economics, and cultures of these peoples. We can show our love for them by being willing to pay taxes for foreign aid, by sharing homes with foreign students or visitors. We can find many ways of showing our love for people in material ways once we are aware of who, in concrete circumstances, our needy brother is.

The demands of the apostolate, which is the same as vital Christian living, force people to live a cut below others of their own class. Many couples engaged in family movements are spending substantial sums annually for baby sitters, additional telephone charges, postage, travel expenses to meetings and conventions. They find themselves more sensitive to the material needs of people presented to them through Church or civic appeals, and to the needs in the neighborhood which only a person with a loving look can discover and which must be subtly alleviated without wounding the pride of the receiver. Their apostolic commitment provides a built-in form of voluntary poverty.

VIII

THE WORTH OF WORK

Many Catholic men admit that the only thing outside their family life that makes sense is what they do for the Church. "I am just putting in time at work. The only thing I do worthwhile outside my family life is what I do as a member of the Legion of Mary." This statement repeated with a thousand variations in words, attitudes, and actions is implicitly a denial of the Incarnation. It is a statement of resignation from the combat in which Christ has enlisted us through Confirmation. It is a bitter defeat for the Christian personally and for the world he is called to bring to its perfection by his witness.

The statement is a denial of the authenticity of lay life by people who consider themselves lay apostles. It creates the image of the Catholic as a man of neurotic fears about the defilement that comes from an encounter with the most stimulating and challenging world that mankind has yet known. It implies a number of attitudes which individually may have great merit but in their limited totality show a disrespect for the Incarnation and a failure to accept Christ's challenge to "be in the world but not of it."

Basically work is viewed by the worker as an economic necessity; it also is acknowledged to have therapeutic side effects. For example, we believe work to be a fulfillment of nature's demand that our mind and body be kept busy lest we become victims of introspection and moral and physical flabbiness. Work, too, is seen by the Christian as purgative. The sinner pays the wages of sin by the sweat of his brow. Hard labor can do for the body what confession does for the spirit. While we can accept work as a just punishment, we can also sublimate or spiritualize our work by a morning offering. Pope John has granted a plenary indulgence for any prayer we say in offering our daily toil to God. Individually these attitudes toward work reflect rewarding facets of daily toil. To work to support a family is an act of virtue. To accept work as an expiation of sin is to show at least a partial understanding of Redemption. The morning offering is at least an attempt to diffuse a divine dimension into a lay or secular task.

Even with these attitudes, however, the worker may still show the fundamental disrespect for work that the desert fathers are reputed to have shown by weaving baskets which they would then unweave again. Here is the same disrespect for work that teachers show for learning when they give lessons to their pupils merely to keep them busy. To offer one's work to God without any consideration of its quality or its place in the total scale of human values is to think that God acts like a thief's "fence" and asks no questions as long as the goods continue to be delivered. The morning offering, or a spirituality of intention, can be a shoddy attempt to store up divine favor for eternity with questionable gifts, as though God were interested in quantity rather than quality.

Work must be viewed positively. It is a participation in the work of creation. God left the minerals in the earth to be extracted by man's labor. He left space unexplored to offer man this exciting adventure after the seas, deserts, and forests had been brought under his domain. The present danger that man may abuse his cocreative power and dangle his atomic, nuclear, and chemical weapons over his fellow man in a genocidal threat does not detract from the never-ceasing wonder of man's partnership with God in the unfolding of creation.

God's insertion into the race of men through His Incarnation gives man's part in the continuation of creation a divine dimension. Christ came into the world to redeem it. All of it has entered His human life—the world's beauty, its wretched misery, its defeats, its hopes. Our Lord's redemption extends beyond spiritual values. The world of men, the lilies of the field, bread, water, physical and spiritual blindness were all touched by Christ. Since the Incarnation, nothing but sin is foreign to the Christian. Nothing escapes the Redemption. If we think of Redemption as something inaugurated by Christ, we see it as a continuing process, like Creation. St. Paul speaks of the fullness of Christ, the Mystical Body, generation after generation working towards a climax. This Body will come to its completion at the Second Coming, the Parousia. We are inclined to think of the end of the world as a fatal moment of destruction and annihilation. But the New Jerusalem is to be formed from the Old. Fire in the biblical sense will purge the world of its impurities, take from it its fragility and transitory nature, and consume or transform what cannot remain. In some way all work well done will remain: the meals well prepared, the pages well typed, the bedpans emptied, the classes taught, the floors swept, the research brought to its completion —all will somehow endure in the New Earth or the New Creation. If then our daily work can become the stuff of the living, pulsing Body of Christ among us, how can we treat it with disdain? How can we treat it with less respect than our prayers and fastings?

By the perfection of our work we are hastening the world to its fulfillment in Christ. Prayer cannot be defined as time snatched from the sordid work of the world, work which interrupts our communion with God. Prayer, rather, must be seen as the continuation of Creation, and this filling out of the Body as it hastens to its fullness can only be a source of unending union with God. Every bed made, potato peeled, or ton of steel poured should be seen as the incense of praise rising above the suburban chimney and the black clouds about the steel mill. De Chardin utters the truth in almost lyrical fashion: "He [God] is waiting for us at every moment in our action, in our work of the moment. He is in some sort at the tip of my pen, my spade, my brush, my needle—of heart and of my thought. By pressing the stroke, the line, or the stitch, on which I am engaged, to its ultimate natural finish, I shall arrive at the ultimate aim towards which my innermost will tends."

When we transfer our incarnational view of work to the bread-and-butter realities of our own work, there are nagging and perplexing doubts which must be considered. There is the immediate difficulty of seeing how my routine job can in any way perfect a world that has been in existence millions of years before me and which may bury me as part of a lost generation. It is easy to see the President of the United States as placing his stamp upon the world as he signs documents of world-shaking import at his desk. But what about the millions of typists and clerks who, while necessary for the work of the decision-making administrators, make no decisions themselves in their purely mechanical tasks?

The ideal we hold up to young people is to find work that gives expression to their unique creative talents. In the history of mankind, however, this has never been a realizable ideal for the majority of people. While automation is removing routine jobs from employment classifications, many jobs will of their nature remain routine, monotonous, and without challenge. Since monotony is built into many jobs and middle-aged people cannot afford to retrain for lower paying but more creative work, there is no alternative to facing up to the suffering which must be accepted and endured with the inner joy of the Christian martyr.

The worker whose routine job offers no creative challenge can find sufficient challenge for his charity in the human relationships he can establish in his shop or office. As a union shop steward he can process in a human way the multiple complaints which monotonous work can bring to the fore. The girl in the midst of a sea of desks in an insurance office can pour the oil of kindness upon the troubled waters of human despair that surge around her desk. In an uncreative job situation, she can by her charity, patience, and understanding help build a human work community that is a replica of the community life of the Holy Trinity.

The complexity of our economic life makes for increased specialization, and this in turn makes it more difficult for us to see our work in relation to the finished product of which it is a part. We are as far removed from the shoemaker who measured the foot and discussed the quality of the material with the customer before he began to make the shoes, as we are from the Neanderthal man. Yet at times we should make conscious efforts to realize how our keeping the files from A to J or our pushing buttons to control the conveyor belts are a contribution to the end product which our company produces.

Even though a car may be used by an unmarried couple as a mobile bedroom, by an intoxicated driver as a lethal weapon, or by a member of a family as an escape from family life, the car should be seen in terms of the great blessings it has brought to mankind. It has brought him to new areas where he can live away from the soot of the crowded city. It unites families scattered over the country. It brings people to see and enjoy the wonders of nature and thus affords relief from the boredom of monotonous work.

God has called the auto worker and car salesman to be his coworkers in helping man to establish a deeper communion with nature and a wider communion with mankind. Workers in other industries should make the effort to see how their industry fits into God's unfinished creation and how it can become the stuff of the unfolding work of Christ's redemption.

How do we deal with work in which the production results in a product that is either a questionable good or an unmitigated evil, or one whose promotion is based on unethical methods? The nuclear research physicist is developing a power which can be used for constructive uses, but can the makers of genocidal bombs find a place for their work in an economy that finds its inspiration in the Sermon on the Mount?

Although such a worker may justify his position casuistically, he may find that nagging feelings of guilt can be a source of unhappiness and tension. He may find that peace will come to him by entering work which he has some assurance will not be a potential destructive force. The salesman who sells useless products to people with severely limited means must either dull his sensitivities or suffer inner anguish. On the contrary, the man whose job is to clean lavatories can find satisfaction in the hygienic service he provides for his patrons. While his job offers low status in a society which gives high status to questionable occupations, it has a genuineness and sincerity to it that can make it rewarding.

Pope John in *Mater et Magistra* offers us this summary of the relationship of work to the Redemption: "When Christians put themselves to work—even if it be in a task of a temporal nature—in conscious union with the divine Redeemer, every effort becomes a continuation of the effort of Jesus Christ and is penetrated with redemptive power: He who abides in me, and I in him, he bears much fruit. It thus becomes a more exalted and more noble labor, one which contributes to a man's personal spiritual perfection, helps to reach out and impart to others on all sides the fruits of Christian redemption. It further follows that the Christian message leavens, as it were, with the ferment of the Gospel the civilization in which one lives and works."

IX

THE POSITIVE POWER OF PENANCE

An incarnational spirituality puts emphasis on positive thinking. It stresses the value of ourselves, of others, of places, and of things. It insists that we must be attached to them. A person without attachment is an inhuman person. He is the person who deals with himself and others without permitting himself to expose his feelings. He is a "beat" who plays it "cool." The person who is detached from human concerns and who is correspondingly detached from the needs of others is a caricature of Christianity. He is a pale and sickly Christian.

An incarnational spirituality views as suspect a layman's flight from the world. It questions his renunciation and asks if it might be a form of cowardice, a refuge from responsibility for things and situations, a backing away from the possibility of involvement or commitment, an unwillingness to accept the defeats and failures which come from possessing and using this world's goods, or a withdrawal from the world before the time which God has appointed.

Although detachment, penance, mortification, and fasting are negative terms, they can express a positive power. Detachment is not a value in itself. It must be seen as a means to a purer form of attachment. The only acceptable reason for renouncing anything is because of a stronger attachment to something that is more human, more in keeping with our providential calling, or more helpful to a greater number of people than the thing renounced. We see it in the student foregoing a Saturday night dance for extra study, or in a Tom Dooley giving up family life for life with the Laotians. But the student who does not go to socials because they are too boring, or the Dooley who does not marry because the demands of family life are too burdensome, are examples of sterile detachment.

If in our stress on the inherent goodness of human relationships, places, and things, we seem to be downgrading detachment, we have always before us the doctrine of the Cross, and the writings and lives of the saints, so clearly marked by ascetic practices. The Scriptures frequently remind us that life is a pilgrimage to the heavenly Jerusalem and that we must conduct ourselves as "strangers and pilgrims." We have heard mission preachers and retreat masters remind us of our Lord's admonition: "What does it profit a man if he gain the whole world and lose his immortal soul?" When we think of St. John of the Cross' figure of speech: "Life is like a night in an uncomfortable inn," we think of a lumpy mattress, insufficient bedcovers, and a drafty room. We are impatient for morning to come. Christian literature is filled with this type of negative admonition. It can hardly be passed off as being an exaggeration by people who feel frustrated in a culture that puts the accent on material things and glorifies comfort.

Asceticism or suffering is necessary, but it must be seen as a liberation. We die (detachment) in order that we may live (disciplined attachment). Our difficulty is not with the Cross but with some of its interpreters. The Cross must be seen as having a liberating effect upon our lives. Christ came to make us free. Freedom from our selfish desires and the slavery of sinful habits cannot be achieved without a passion and death of our own. Suffering, which is synonymous with detachment, should be seen as a form of purification, a way to freedom of the spirit.

Unfortunately, for many the Cross is a symbol of sadness and repression. In reality it is a symbol of self-confrontation wherein we face ourselves and in the process transcend ourselves. Self-confrontation is not a term derived from a particular school of clinical psychology or psychiatric analysis; it is the Christian's answer to the challenge of St. Paul: "If you live according to the flesh you shall die; but if by the Spirit you mortify the deeds of the flesh you shall live" (Rom. 15:8). The Cross is not a way of escaping reality, but of facing up to it.

The Cross is also a sign of victory over weakness; it leads us to a fuller life in Christ. Through detachment we can say: "I live now not I but Christ lives in me." This is another way of stating Christ's reminder that unless the seed die it will not live. Self-indulgence cannot stand in the way of the apostolate. The disciple of Christ must purge from his life any obstacle to his growth in love or his particular vocation. St. Paul put it in more blunt words: "I chastise my body and bring it into subjection lest perhaps when I have preached to others, I myself should become a castaway" (1 Cor. 9:27).

Work is one of the great sources of detachment. Devotion to duty demands that we overcome inertia. The alarm clock, the backlog of unfinished business, the whining child, the lesson which has to be given over and over again with the slow learner are forms of discipline which demand that we rise above our natural inclinations and lovingly accept the demands of the moment. The monotony of work can be overcome by trying to see new depths in what we are doing or in the people with whom we are associated. Unless the work is entirely mechanical there should be willingness to venture an added and creative dimension to our lives. Creativeness demands detachment. It means parting company with long-established and comfortable habits or ruts without knowing what the experiment will yield or what new demands it will make upon our way of life.

"Anyone whose aim is conquering the earth . . . has surely begun to take leave of himself at the same time as taking possession of himself," writes de Chardin. "This is also true of the man who rejects mere enjoyment, the line of least resistance, the easy possession of things and ideas, and sets courageously on the path of work, inward renewal, and the ceaseless broadening and purification of his ideal. And it is true, again, of the man who has given his time, his health, or his life to something greater than himself—a family to be supported, a country to be saved, a truth to be discovered, a cause to be defended. All these men are continually passing from attachment to detachment as they faithfully mount the ladder of human endeavor."

Work helps purge the mind of self-pity, sexual fantasies, and self-defeating introspection. Without work we would have time to brood over imagined injustices perpetrated upon us by fellow men. However, our devotion to work has to be disciplined. The man who remains in his office after all the other employees have left may be using work as an escape from his family or other social responsibilities. A person can become neurotically attached to his work, justifying himself on the basis of work's fundamental holiness. The more holy the object the more subtle are our rationalizations. Life is all of a piece; therefore work must submit itself to the discipline that regulates the whole.

Family life is a school of detachment. The child who is a victim of "momism" is the child of a mother who is overattached. The father who cannot be distracted from his newspaper and TV program to discipline his children or help them with their schoolwork is too detached. Usually the basic source of the lack of balance in the parent-child relationship is the husband-wife relationship. Healthy conjugal love is based on a delicate balance between detachment and attachment. An infatuation is an undisciplined attachment which can become true conjugal love only through detachment. Detachment in conjugal love is not a form of monastic or clerical celibacy. It is refined, sensitive attachment, and is a means of achieving fulfillment.

If the pleasurable experience of love-making is to be a genuine attachment, it cannot be carried out selfishly, through exploitation of the partner. A debt paid in justice is not likely to be an act of true love. True love seeks the pleasure of both the lover and the beloved, but is always ready to forego pleasure for the sake of the other or for some greater good that will accrue to the marriage and the Church. The detachment comes from a sympathetic understanding of the needs and responses of the other. It demands a ruthless purging of selfish desires in the interest of an attraction that transcends two self-centered people. At one time it may demand the asceticism of St. Anthony in the desert wrestling with the devil in the practice of sexual abstinence; at another time the giving up of oneself to the other without reserve and without a martyr complex when one feels no urgent desire for any sexual expression of love.

When a person in comfortable economic circumstances hears the call to an apostolic life, he is bothered about the admonitions of our Lord to deny oneself and embrace a spirit of poverty. Can we possess and enjoy unlimited possessions and be poor in spirit? The state of material poverty is not necessarily a form of detachment. The monk is aware of the religious who violates the spirit of poverty by clinging to his useless trinkets like priceless treasure. The layman is aware of the legitimacy and necessity of possessions. The question is how he can possess them without being possessed by them. One test comes in dealing with the poor. Can we meet them on equal terms and gladly visit them in their own surroundings without a patronizing, condescending, or hostile attitude? Our confrontation with the poor shows up our feelings about our own possessions.

In Latin the word for baggage is *impedimenta*. It describes well the burden of possessions. They have a power of impeding our social mobility. We must look around ourselves occasionally to see what we might be able to do without, lest it impede our journey. Traveling lightly is an aid to clear thinking as well as easy moving. The person who lives on an upper middle-income level should adopt the ascetic practice of visiting the other side of the tracks, to identify occasionally with the poor in travel accommodations and restaurants. If we have been liberated from grinding poverty, we should thank God, but we also need to feel and be aware of the universal presence of poverty in the world before we can consider ourselves "poor in spirit." There must be some real identification with the people who are poor in fact, and this requires something other than a vague wishing them well.

The greatest form of detachment and the safest form of mortification or penance is to permit ourselves to be imposed upon. There can be little place for self when others are determining the disposal of our time and resources. It is simply complying with our Lord's injunction to go the extra mile. In this way, we give to others the determination of our penitential practices. We permit those in need to be our masters. We must distinguish, however, between the person who freely follows this way of life and the neurotic who is unable to say "no" to the requests of others because he fears the possibility of rejection by the person he is refusing.

The married couple who operate their household with an open-door policy are teaching the entire family the spirit of detachment and penance. The stability of their married life and their proven generosity in the neighborhood will bring the lonely and poor in spirit to their door. Each guest will be greeted and treated as Christ. People in every neighborhood are always asking St. Peter's question, "To whom shall we go?" In the ordinary course of events, their way to Christ will be through the family who receives them as Christ.

The hair shirt, the discipline, and chains are not the tools of a penitential life for the layman today. His stigmata might well be ulcers or a coronary. Attending meetings, faithfully carrying out group assignments, offering one's services cheerfully for extra chores are ways of continuing the passion of our Lord in one's own life. The work of the apostolate can be, at times, so demanding that nothing less than the carrying of the Cross can be adequate motivation to continue. The absence of this motivation is the obvious explanation of apathy. Eventually the people must see the difficulties of lay life as apostolic penances equivalent to St. Paul's shipwrecks, sleepless nights, fastings, and every manner of trial.

If a layman has a rigorous set of ascetic practices which do not stem from the exigencies of his commitment to lay life, it might be a clue that he is leading a double life. It might be that there is something about his occupational or professional or family life which he refuses to face in a Christian way and that he is attempting to assuage his guilt feelings by ascetic practices which do not challenge his defenses.

The mother of a large family who is deeply enmeshed in civic and apostolic projects knows the kinds of sacrifice the modern lay apostle is called upon to make. Because of her new way of life she gradually loses the sympathetic understanding of her parents, relatives, and long-standing friends. They cannot understand why she is so busy and has so many interests which have no relation to her family. Besides the loss of approval of her relatives and older friends is the loss of status. She finds that she has dropped one notch in the carefully coded class system of our "classless" society.

One such mother offers the following as examples of the sacrifice of pride, time, and money which her commitment to Christ in lay life demands: beer and punch instead of a well-equipped bar; cookies and coffee instead of smorgasbord for Christmas open house; fifty-nine-cent stockings, worn with runs, instead of a name brand; suits a little shinier; sheets unironed and when torn made into crib sheets and drapery linings, T shirts and finally, handkerchiefs. The sacrifices she lists for husbands are giving up a bowling league, a card club, or Saturday golf. For some it might be TV movies or mystery stories. Each cultural group demands a different form of sacrifice. The reality of the pinch is the same. Another sacrifice for this mother was the feeling of smugness and respectability that membership in her former little in-group permitted. Now she can no longer share and accept the clichés that let her off the hook of responsibility. She must give up forever the easy out of "Yes, but what can I do about it?" She must give up the luxury of never challenging accepted ideas, jokes, decisions. The reward for her sacrifices she names as "sharing the great works of Christ in our times." There is no life of charity without facing and accepting the spiritual and material detachment it demands.

X

FREEDOM TO LOVE

I once dramatized the story of the Prodigal Son in a retreat to high-school senior boys. A young man reaches his majority. He is attracted by the bright lights of the big city. He asks for his legal share of the family estate. His father, who is a wise and loving parent, realizes that his son will not be able to cope with the catastrophic moral situations of this totally different and dangerous way of life. He has a number of alternatives in meeting the just demands of his son. He can lecture his son on the evils of neon-light living. He can use legal devices to tie up the boy's inheritance for a number of months or years. He can threaten his son by telling him that, if he goes, he will never be welcome back. Or he can give the money gladly, with a smile, his blessing, and an affectionate farewell. Because the father respects the son's God-given human dignity and right to determine the direction of his life, he chooses the last course. He does it with the foreknowledge that the son will abuse his freedom. So also, God, in giving us free will, gives us the power to reject Him. He loves us so much that He permits us to reject His advances as a lover. Freedom is an essential condition for love.

The young man is enthralled by his new way of life—beer, booze, and B girls—which he mistakenly thinks is freedom.

Before his money is spent, he begins to wonder if the freedom of the big city is a form of slavery and the slavery of the home life he left really an atmosphere for true freedom. But he is in no mood for philosophical distinctions. As long as he has money in his pocket or in his checking account, he can drive away these depressing thoughts about the home he left. Then his financial resources dry up, and the barmaids refuse to patronize him, the prostitutes look upon him with contempt, and the tavern owners threaten to call the police if he does not leave peaceably at once.

He does not think about going home because he will not admit to himself that he erred. He lacks the humility to face his father and ask forgiveness. So he seeks a job. In a depressed area he finds an employer who welcomes him as an employee because of his youthful energy. There is no salary attached to the job—he gets only his keep. He is given complete responsibility for cleaning the entire fifth floor of a skid row "hotel." For food, he shares the leftovers of the ground floor beanery with other workers. For a room he has an empty cubicle on his floor.

He can go no lower than a skid row existence. His defenses crumble. He admits failure to himself. Now he is willing to think about returning to his father's house. He is too proud to desire complete forgiveness. He would be satisfied with clean bedding and a place at the servants' table in return for an honest day's work. How could he think about complete acceptance by his father! He does not even have title in justice to employment as a hired hand. As he turns the last bend in the road, he sees his father. They embrace and tears of joy run freely down the cheeks of both men. The obvious lesson here is the return to divine life of the sinner-son who grovelled in the muck of subhuman living. We see the prodigious folly of God's prodigality.

After telling them this story, I next asked the seniors to image the situation wherein a fellow is trying to sneak into his home at 2:00 A.M. Sunday morning. He betrays himself by his unsure footing, topples over a chair, and arouses his father.

The father smells the liquor from his clothing and from his brewery breath. He sees the lipstick smeared on his son's collar. My question was simply, "Would your father, in these circumstances, treat you as the Father treated the Prodigal Son?" I paused for reflection and studied the facial reactions before me. Finally, there was a burst of laughter. The spontaneous response in words amounted to: "How ridiculous can you be, Father? My father would take me apart limb by limb."

If the boys' reaction is any indication, we give our own prodigal son stories unhappy endings, and use them to prove that freedom should be withheld. But even the real prodigal son story sometimes has an unhappy ending. Not every sinner returns to the Father's house. Does this destroy the Father's grant of freedom? Or is freedom a value in itself to be given for no other reason than that the person may be treated as a being with the right to determine his own destiny? Freedom is a two-edged sword. We give it out of love, even though by so doing we permit others to destroy themselves as God permits us to choose an eternity of hell.

From experience with parents I find that this paradox of freedom in discipline—and discipline in freedom—is not understood. When I state my position of freedom for children within the framework of order or discipline, I am accused of hedging and double talk. Their remarks imply that freedom is irreconcilable with the firm hand of authority. In defense I plead that Christianity is filled with paradoxes. It is a life of both joy and sorrow, dying and living at the same time, of giving and receiving simultaneously. It is a life of tensions. A paradox sets up a tension, and the resolution of tensions makes life exciting and challenging. When a man and woman marry, by the very fact of being opposites biologically and psychologically, they set up a tension. It is not the ignoring or the destruction of opposite characteristics but the disciplining or harnessing of the tension resulting from them that makes possible creative activity.

Freedom is not license. It requires training, but it also requires elbow room for failure. With children there must be an understanding or tolerance for rebellion against authority as well as for the abuse of privileges or freedom. This can be reconciled with the firm and sure hand of authority which guides without dominating or destroying the personality of the child. Parental authority which presents high but reasonable goals to a child without forcing acceptance of them heightens the child's realization of its own inherent human dignity. There are no rules or books which cover each child's stages of development. Child guidance is an art which parents can achieve only by trial and error. While they strive to achieve balance, they must always settle for something less than perfection in the art of raising children who will be both free and obedient, docile and aggressive.

A mother of nine small children told me how she took her three-year-old shopping. Before leaving the store she decided that her budget allowed for the purchase of a ten-cent knick-knack for the child. She picked something from the counter which she thought the child would like. Before she gave it to him it dawned upon her that the child was capable of deciding what object on the ten-cent counter he preferred. Here was respect for freedom by a strong and loving parent who could distinguish between the necessary use of parental authority and the God-given liberty of the child. The example has even wider ramifications than respect for freedom. In such ways does a child learn to make decisions. Possibilities for similar experiences in freedom and decision-making are many: clothes to be worn, games to be played, food to be chosen from the restaurant menu.

A parent of teen-agers remarks that all she expects from her children is order in the home. They are expected to contribute to the work of the household and abide by directives which have not been arbitrarily made but which are necessary for the common good of a venture in family living. Clothes are to be hung up. Youngsters are to help with the meals and be reasonably punctual. Their minds, their thoughts and the direction of their lives are their own. Readers will quarrel with the last sentence, but it is to be understood not as recommending abdication of parental concern for the child's thoughts, desires, and expectations, but as in favor of a healthy respect for the most precious possession of the child, its power to choose. Without this kind of freedom, the child will never be able to give or receive genuine love.

It is an abdication of parental responsibility to establish in the family a democratic order which permits every child over five not only to have an equal voice in all decisions but to have veto power in all matters the child considers might adversely affect him. However, within the framework of a reasonable and flexible regime, there is room for the development of the personality of each through a maximum use of freedom. Children need not only the inner security that comes from order and discipline but also the inner freedom that comes from the kind of respect the father of the Prodigal Son had for his restless child.

Education has been cynically defined as the process of handing down the prejudices of one generation to another. Both parents and teachers must continually try to objectify their feelings to see if they are presenting truth (or opinion) as something to be freely accepted or rejected or whether they are using it as a weapon and applying refined methods of brainwashing to gain assent to it. Parents and teachers have their subtle methods of manipulating minds. Often it is those who cry loudest against political forms of slavery who, in their methods to get their point across, use demagoguery or unwarranted fear to force conviction.

As a high-school teacher who dealt with parents for sixteen years, I learned to assess the true feelings of parents in regard to their children's human dignity. When a parent says, "I do not expect my son to lead his class," you pay no attention to the words but to the feelings expressed. If the statement is made casually, you take it at its face value. If the statement is made with deep feeling, you feel that the son is under tremendous pressure to reach the top. It may help the parents to explain to them how a boy may develop hostile feelings toward overbearing parents and may punish them by refusing to do even average work.

Parents are quick to affirm that their children are free to

choose their own way of life, think their own thoughts, and choose their own friends as they grow older. Yet parents betray themselves not only by the inflection of their voices but also by the practical and delicate manipulation of conversation and by behind-the-scene maneuvers. The autocratic parent who lays down the party line for the entire family in blunt terms does less harm to a child's freedom than the manipulating parent who prattles about freedom. If the child can easily identify the source of his loss of freedom, he can realistically rebel against it and thus be saved at the core of his being. It is the unseen enemy who destroys him.

From parents and all others, Christianity requires the delicate balance of a tightrope walker. If purgatory and indulgences are overstressed, the power of the sacrament of last anointing is underestimated. If hell and God's justice are overplayed, His mercy is underplayed. If purity is stressed as the all-important virtue, charity will be dethroned as the queen of virtues. If obedience alone is sought or demanded of children, freedom, love, and creativity will not be nourished.

In this country, Catholics are accused by their adversaries of adhering to an authoritarian Church. Catholics pride themselves on their obedience to Church law. It seems that we could re-examine our approach to freedom, since Christ came to set us free. The Catholic should be the prime champion of freedom and creativity since both pertain to the essence of God's nature. The ascetic life should be discussed in terms of liberation or freedom. Obedience should be seen as a way toward true freedom for one's self, not as an end in itself. The obedience demanded should be reasonable and aimed at the individual good as well as the common good. External order in a school or a home can be deceptive. It can conceal repressed, hostile feelings and it may be suppressing individual talents. An external order should never be more than is necessary to help true development and the internalization of order in the life of the individual.

The parent and the schoolteacher should encourage intellectual curiosity by raising questions. Creativity in the learning process can only be developed in an atmosphere that is neither dogmatic nor moralistic. The parent or teacher who unceasingly repeats dogmatic truths and formulas, for study and memorization, may be peforming a service, but is not preparing a climate friendly to the spirit. Such a parent or teacher tends to produce dull, standardized, unimaginative Christians who have a dogged fidelity to a narrow concept of duty. Training for freedom is always a messy, untidy task. And it is most discouraging to find that the training is often unwanted by the people who plead to be set free.

The entire teen-age American culture is seldom judged in any deeper terms than dirty comic books, plunging necklines, passionate kissing, going steady and heavy drinking. Problems in these areas are solved with prohibitions. There is little patience for a longer look and for dealing with life as a whole. Capsule answers are satisfying to the simple, but they never prepare people to meet life on its own terms. Only the self-reliant Catholic who has learned that he must assume responsibility for his own moral decisions can live an intelligent Christian life in our society.

Self-reliance demands reading and discussion, trial and error, in a climate of intellectual freedom and trust by priests, teachers and parents who are involved in the formation of youth. The teen-ager who said he wished that Christ had written a gospel on dating summed up the subject. This high-school senior preferred packaged answers to facility in making delicate decisions and the ability to live by them.

The decade of the sixties, with its dialogue between hierarchy and laity on clerical-lay relationships, shows a more mature concept of freedom within the Church in America. The ancestor of today's middle-class American Catholic was the unwanted foreigner. He clung to the hem of the priest's cassock in seeking protection and patronage. He showed his appreciation for these services by his docility and obedience to the priest, and by his generous contribution of money—and even of sons and daughters, who entered seminaries and convents in large numbers—to the Church. His attitude was laudable in its setting.

With a laity which is climbing fast in social and economic status and is achieving ever-higher levels of education, the continuation of this paternalistic relationship between laity and clergy can only spell disaster. Pope Pius XII was pleading for freedom for the laity within the framework of obedience when, in a speech in 1950 to the Catholic Press, he called for a "public opinion within the Church." He said that "there would be something missing from her life if there were no public opinion within her, a defect for which pastors as well as the faithful would be responsible. . . ."

It would be a mistake to think that the laity are pleading universally for more freedom. A plea for freedom is an implicit request to assume responsibility. Many lay people raise their passivity and timidity to the level of obedience. They rationalize that they become "more Catholic" to the degree that they ask no questions and forfeit their freedom. The following are two random examples: The president of home-school association calls the pastor to get his permission to change the color of the raffle tickets from green to blue. The president of a young adults organization, in commenting on a seeming irrational decision laid down by a newly ordained assistant, says, "Father didn't give a reason, and of course, I didn't ask for one." In both cases the layman chose the easy course of childish dependence. To indict the laity for their overdependence is not to absolve the clergy of all guilt for continuation of this relationship. Both must learn that the give and take of discussion, as painful as the encounter may be, is the only therapy for a relationship that has frozen into a rigid pattern.

For many people, freedom means escape from themselves. There are many escape routes: travel, tranquilizers, TV—anything used purely as a distraction. True freedom, however, is a staying-with oneself. It is an acceptance of oneself, of one's providential circumstances in life, of one's built-in limitations. The source of our servitude or slavery is within us. If humility is basically self-acceptance, then the way to freedom is through humility. The responsible use of freedom is another term for acceptance of oneself.

Obedience makes us free when we appreciate and freely accept it. When we *freely* submit to the true need of another, we are obeying ourselves. We are answering the call of our true and better selves. Real freedom must be obedience to one's true self. The layman who remarked that his greatest form of penance was responding to the needs of others wherever he found them is a man of both obedience and freedom. Like St. Vincent de Paul, he permits the needs of others to be his most demanding master. In freely responding to the needs of others, he is responding to the needs of his true self, which is linked with the fate of every human creature on the face of the earth. In responding to the plaintive cries of human need and misery, he is building up the Body of Christ. It is thus in, through, and with Christ that he achieves his freedom as a human being and a son of God.

The layman who desires to fulfill his vocation as a Christian witness or apostle must have this appreciation of the freedom of a son of God. He may have to overcome a childhood religious training which emphasized formality, sterile obedience, and conformity to outmoded and meaningless practices. He will have to shed his defensiveness and insecurity as a Catholic layman and gladly meet the world on its own terms, thinking of it not as an adversary but as a challenger, or a lover to be wooed.

Lay Catholics will never make an impact in society until they begin to apply freshly the Gospel to daily practice. This requires a different approach to training Catholics than the typical catechetical methods used thus far. Ways must be found to develop a mature, autonomous, responsible Catholic layman. He must be taught to appreciate freedom as a hallmark of a son of God. He must embrace obedience to his true self and the never-relenting demands of his vocation. Thus, he will be imitating the freedom and obedience of Christ. He said, in reference to His freedom, "I will lay down My life." St. Paul summarizes His obedience: "He was obedient unto death, even the death of the Cross." Because He acted freely, He obeyed Himself in His death.

XI

THE MEANING OF THE MASS

Sunday Mass for a Catholic is often characterized by a mad dash to be there on time. The layman whom we caricature wants to sleep as late as he can, be properly dressed, have his Sunday envelope in his pocket, his Sunday missal in the glove compartment of the car, his car keys in his hand as he closes the door behind him, and hopes to find a space in the parking lot not too far removed from the church entrance. As he enters the church he picks up a Sunday bulletin and looks for a seat not too close to the front of a nearly full church.

The priest, with his back turned to the congregation, is engaged with the altar boy in the prayers at the foot of the altar. Our layman has the option of giving the parish bulletin the once-over or finding his place in his missal. After five minutes of kneeling and standing he sits down to listen to the priest in the pulpit. The announcements are less than exciting. It is a litany of times of Masses, notices of deaths and marriages, past and forthcoming collections, and a variety of items of common knowledge or of little relevance to him. The suggested sermon topics for the month in his diocese may very well be sterilization, abortion, mercy killing, and Peter's Pence. It is more likely that these topics will gripe him than grip him.

If Masses are on the hour, there is the consoling thought that whatever the subject, the priest will be out of the pulpit by twenty after the hour. After the sermon, the celebrant turns his back again to the congregation and our man has ten minutes of holy boredom, interrupted only by the bells or the antics of a child or a noseblower; then there is the trek to the communion rail. In a large parish two or three priests will ply their way back and forth quickly but reverently along the rail. This done, the tabernacle door is closed, and after a few minutes of purifications and prayers the congregation is released to the pure light of day. There is the relief of a duty done, the best part of an hour given weekly to God.

Given the difficulties of trying to typify the Mass participation of forty-three million American Catholics, is this honest reporting? While many of the Mass habits listed are distinctly American, such as driving to Mass in a car, the attitudes may have a greater universality than at first appears. Cardinal Lercaro of Bologna, speaking from a wider perspective than the American, says that Sunday Mass is like a cafeteria. People are gathered in the same place at the same time, and are eating the same food, but they are not doing it together.

The Cardinal's complaint is not about efficiency or lack of it, but that, at Mass, we are not a family; and worse, that we have no awareness that we should be. Who thinks on Sunday morning as he elbows his way to the altar rail that he is making his way to the family table? Who is aware that the Eucharist is more than an innoculation against temptations to impurity or a booster shot of grace to build up our spiritual muscles for an encounter with the enemy? Who is aware that Sunday Mass, which is a remembrance of the Last Supper, is the trysting place with God where we feast in the Lord with His and our brethren?

I recently visited a newly founded suburban parish which does not fit the stereotype. St. Florian's is being stamped in the image of the pastor's concept of the Eucharist and of his own role as pastor. He sees himself as the leader of a Eucharistic community. In this view he is the anointed and appointed leader of his parishioners in their worship of our heavenly Father through Christ, our elder brother. Although he is harassed with debts, landscaping, insurance underwriting, furnishing a new church and rectory, and countless other administrative details of setting a new parish in motion, he cares for the sick, the needy, the instruction of children (without the aid of a Catholic school), prepares converts, seeks out the strays, and deals with the paper work involved in validating marriages. In this welter of spiritual and material anxieties, he never loses sight of his primary pastoral role, as he conceives it, of bringing all people and things to a head through Christ's sacrificial worship of His Father.

Sunday morning at St. Florian's reflects the pastor's orientation to the priesthood and the direction in which he is gently but firmly leading his flock in worship. The enclosed foyer of the church was designed as a parish hall later to be converted into classrooms. Presently it serves the function of the plaza in the Latin American village where people congregate before and after Mass and for other community affairs. St. Florian's large foyer is the parish's public square where people meet before and after parish services and engage in the small talk and serious discussions which are the cement of a human community. At St. Florian's the human and divine are not separated at Mass time. By exchanging informal greetings before Mass, the people are preparing themselves for their great family action at God's holy table. After Mass their greetings in the social hall and parking lot are the warmer for their having feasted on the one Bread which makes the Body one.

Before Mass on Sunday those who will receive the Body of the Lord in Communion come to a table outside the sanctuary where they find wafers of bread which they place in a ciborium on the table. These breads, symbolizing the gift of their lives, become, through the action of the Mass, divine life for them. When the ushers at the Offertory bring these breads to the altar, the people are able to see in this ceremony the dedication of their week of work in the city, in the homes, in the school—the joy of life being caught up in Christ's giving of Himself in the renewal of His glorious sacrificial offering. It is a forceful reminder that in the action of the Mass the Word is taking the flesh of St. Florian's parishioners for His continuous sacrifice of praise to His Heavenly Father.

The housewife's sink of dishes or tub of diapers, her hairdresser's appointment, her latest entry on the social calendar, punishments meted out to unruly children, are symbolized in the gesture of placing the host in the ciborium and participate in Christ's prolongation of His redemptive act as it is renewed each Sunday at St. Florian's. God's love and man's response as a member of a redeemed community are joined in Christ's weekly saving action in this section of American suburbia.

A decree was issued from Rome in September, 1958, that the laity be given back their place in vocal participation in every low Mass they offer with the priest. The decree has met with something less than an enthusiastic response. In many parishes the children singsong the responses; in others the adults respond in muted and doleful tones which could be interpreted as a cry of despair, "Will they ever leave us alone, at least in God's house?" Some experts in the field of worship say the trouble is with the language. They deplore the efforts to make a dead language the carrier of life. The more they see a despairing flock on Sunday stumble over *consubstantialem Patri* the more they cry for these parts to be permitted in the vernacular. Whatever the merits of the vernacular, we are mistaken if we think a common language is our most basic need. Children can singsong their prayers in English and adults can prefer silence to a response in English to a liturgical greeting or prayer in English. Singing together and praying together must be preceded by, or at least supported by, a conviction that we are one family in Christ, that we are God's holy people in a deeper sense than were the Jews. Vernacular in the liturgy needs the support that is anchored in a faith which sees Baptism as an incorporation into God's holy family, or Christ's Mystical Body.

The pastor of St. Florian's does not spend his time bewailing the Church's slowness in responding to the avant-garde's lamentations. He prefers to spend his time teaching the people English hymns which set to easy melody the theology of the Eucharist and emphasize our oneness in Christ's Mystical Body through partaking of the Bread that makes us one. Instead of using his time in the pulpit to moralize about aspects of our Christian heritage which are part of the common store of knowledge and accepted ethics, he spends the time in pointing out the implications in our daily life of our Baptism, Confirmation, and the Eucharist.

Can the social aspects of the Eucharist be taught in our Catholic schools and our Confraternity of Christian Doctrine classes? I am sure that in every course on the Mass the point is made that the liturgy is a form of public worship. It can be simply presented. When the priest acts, it is the one Christ, the only Mediator, who acts for the entire Church. When a priest offers Mass even without a server, it is the whole Church which offers the Mass. It is at this precise juncture that our great failure lies. This is all intellectual gymnastics until we weave it into the fabric of our entire life. Through our theological teaching people come to know *about* the Church, but fail to know the Church experientially. The knowledge is academic rather than vital. While it is unfair to place the blame for lack of liturgical experience upon the classroom teacher, it is unrealistic to put all our eggs in an educational system, as American Catholics are prone to do. The Church in St. Paul's time welded emotional feelings, theological concepts, and human solidarity into a living religious experience. Every reader, I am sure, has had at some time this experiential sense of the Mass as an expression of a living community in Christ.

Some time ago I attended a priests' convention at which there was a shortage of altars and chalices for the saying of Mass. A few priests decided to set up a portable altar in a small room where they could celebrate a community Mass with English hymns, a homily, and Offertory and Communion processions. We stood with our missals only a few feet from the celebrant. Celebrating Mass in this way, at a time when we were living a common life and sharing with each other our deepest thoughts, our lightest moments, and our commitment to a specific work of the Mystical Body, enabled us to experience the Mass as a family action.

A few months previous to this priests' meeting I was asked to speak at a Young Christian Students' college study day. The talk, the small-group discussions, and the reports dealt with the college student's responsibility as a member of the Mystical Body to the international order. There was much discussion of Latin America, the Peace Corps, and the Papal Volunteers.

This session was climaxed by a community Mass. This Mass was as different an experience from a typical parish Mass as day is from night. A oneness in Christ had been created through the free exchange of thoughts about the degree and kind of commitment the students were ready to make for Christ in Latin America. There was a dimension to the participation which defies description and which somehow expressed a collective commitment to Christ through this liturgical action. There was real community in spite of the fact that the Mass was in Latin, there was no Offertory procession, and that we used the Roman rite which scholars claim has a clerical or monastic orientation. The odds were obviously heavy against a meaningful community experience, but our oneness in Christ was felt strongly enough to break through encrusted forms which were designed to express the sentiments of a people whose way of life and experiences were far removed from ours.

At another time I slipped incognito into a Sunday evening revival meeting to see if the Pentecostals had anything to teach the liturgical movement by way of meaningful community participation. (In Brazil and Chile the Pentecostals are the largest Protestant body, and in South Africa the second largest. In the United States, while they rank twenty-seventh numerically, they claim to be fifth in the number of foreign missionaries.) When I entered the meeting I thought I was at a Young Christian Students' high school study week. The congregation was singing with its hands. There was a spontaneity to the singing and hand-clapping but not the enthusiasm of the YCSers singing with their voices and hands "Dem Bones Will Rise Again." The ages of the groups made the difference.

Since I could not join the revivalists, I left shortly. I could not escape the conclusion that a revival meeting, a YCS study day, or a song fest with appropriate tunes would make a good preparation for a community Mass. Silence is best appreciated after outbursts of speech and song. Basic to the revivalist and YCS enthusiasm was a common commitment to Christ. This does not come by the simple handing out of song sheets. It requires prior soul-searching and sacrifice.

The examples used thus far have been about communities structured around a common goal which they were able to discuss freely in small and intimate groups. Is it possible to establish this psychological expression of our oneness in Christ in a vast American cathedral filled with people who have never met before? Such an experience I shared in Philadelphia's Cathedral of SS. Peter and Paul on the occasion of the visit of Cardinal Rugambwa of Tanganyika to the city of brotherly love. The dialogue Mass offered by the Cardinal with a crowd that filled the seating and standing room capacity to overflowing was a breakthrough for the cause of interracial love and the liturgical movement. Here was a healthy mixture of races singing English hymns and responding to and joining with their African brother in Christ. One could sense the cohesiveness of this community.

Curiosity seekers turning out to see an African cardinal do not form a real community. These people, on the contrary, without verbalizing their thoughts, had turned out to identify themselves with the aspirations of the emerging African nations and the local cause of interracial justice and love. This was evident in their vocalized participation in the Eucharistic service. Can this experience be repeated in our Sunday Masses in our great urban areas? These Masses by their nature suffer from routine. Even an African Cardinal offering such a Mass every Sunday would suffer the loss of enthusiastic response which goes with novelty. An ingenious pastor and willing parishioners convinced that the Eucharist is a family affair can, within the framework of present liturgical legislation, take giant strides towards making the Mass a foretaste of the Trinitarian love of which the Eucharist is a pledge. This pledge will be redeemed on the condition that we set love in motion in the vast network of human relations which enmeshes us.

In this chapter I have stressed the communal aspects of the Mass. My effort has been to redress the lack of balance in the view which sees the Christian's life in God as a "Jesus and me" dialogue during which "the rest of the world can go hang." Another unbalanced view is to see the liturgy as a sacred action removed from the stresses and strains of both one's personal and social life. In this view the Mass is the renewal of Christ's death and rising at which the Catholic is a witness, as were Mary and John at the foot of the Cross and the soldiers at the tomb, but without any responsibility for carrying out its implications in daily life. The Mass can be a perfectly executed sacred drama which fails to draw our lives into its embrace.

Our attitude towards distractions at Mass may give us a clue to how well we integrate our daily lives with the liturgical action at the altar. One morning at Mass I was distracted. A telephone call the night before had disturbed me, and now was on my mind during the Consecration of the Mass. Then it occurred to me that the call was not a foreign substance and that I should consecrate it, that I should dip it into the Precious Blood. The call was about a matter that had serious repercussions on lives of many people; it created an anxiety within me which deprived me of a restful night of sleep. Such events are part of my real life which I should accept lovingly and without the support of tranquilizers. At Mass time I should not consider them as distractions or weeds in the garden of my memory. If they insist on taking their place on the paten or in the chalice, I accept them lest the Mass be for me a technically well-executed but lifeless ritual.

As a scriptural basis for bringing our cares and anxieties to Mass I submit St. Paul's description of Baptism in Romans, chapter six. There he says that if, through Baptism, we have been dipped or plunged into Christ's death and rising, then at Mass our present lives should be consciously dipped or plunged into this present renewal of Christ's death and rising. Each day we can make this subjective living out of our Baptism in the stream of life encounter the objective renewal of Christ's life as it gloriously unfolds on the altar.

The theologian in developing a thesis moves from the Scriptures to the Fathers of the Church. I offer the cryptic sentence of St. Cyprian to support the necessary relationship of the Mass to our personal struggle with the vicissitudes of life. "The sacrifice of the Lord is not complete as far as our sanctification is concerned, unless our offering and sacrifices correspond to His Passion."

The Mass for the layman is the bridge between his lay life, which he touches by his presence, and the Lord of creation. The layman exercises his priestly baptismal character when he acts as mediator for his milieu at Mass. In a lecture on lay spirituality to priests, a layman had this to say: "The layman never goes alone to Mass. He brings himself, his family, his neighbors, the paperboy, the milkman, the man who drives the bus that takes him to work, his fellow workers, the things they do and the things they make, the people they sell to, the people they buy from—in short, he brings all the world with its people and its institutions with which he has contact in his daily and routine life. In this regard he has a unique role at the Mass. It is unique with respect to the priest because the priest has contact with this part of the world only through the layman."

XII

"PRAY WITHOUT CEASING"

In this country Protestants and Catholics have engaged in a healthy rivalry in turning out crowds. Whether it is a CYO national convention or a Billy Graham Crusade, thoughtful people ask themselves what happens to the youthful enthusiasm or the decisions for Christ when people are back home engaged in their pedestrian way of life. The people who arrange a convention or a priest who conducts a retreat see the people leave in the clouds, convinced that they will never forget this landmark in their lives and pledging themselves to their convention or retreat resolutions with an undying determination. The social engineer knows without any touch of cynicism that enthusiasm follows the laws of nature, that what goes up must come down.

The thoughtful person wants to know the content of the enthusiasm. Was the basic message an appeal to our highest reason and our deepest faith or were the people under the unceasing barrage of an emotional assault which produced sentimental or irrational convictions? Will the rally, convention, or retreat leave the conventioneer or retreatant with a firmer grasp of reality after the emotional fervor has subsided? The same question could be posed by the reader of this book. Have the emotional, rational, and spiritual blended into genuine motivation? If we can answer affirmatively to these questions about rallys, retreats, or books, there remains still another question. How is religious conviction sustained? The answer is luminously simple: unceasing prayer.

Apostolic action comes to a grinding halt when the apostle ceases to pray. His work may go on and even become technically and organizationally more perfect but the foundation is weakening in proportion to his alienation from prayer. Placards and banners, organizational charts and better office procedures can never replace prayer. Prayer is the wellspring of apostolic action. When the well dries up, the apostolate and the apostle will die. Meetings and conferences will be arranged to diagnose and arrest the malignancy. Unless the truth about prayer is faced, there will be complaints and bitterness about the obstacles to the work, lack of cooperation in high and low places, and the perverse unwillingness of others to see things the right way. There will be resolutions and new committees charged with finding gimmicks instead of soul-searching answers.

The Christian prays not because he is a member of a Catholic or Protestant apostolic group but because he is a creature who has been redeemed by Christ and has committed himself to Him by Baptism. The Christian prays because prayer is the ordinary form of communication with God and an expression of his love and union with God. Prayer has the same ultimate purpose for the Christian as does serving one's neighbor. Each is a path to the love of God. The individual Christian does not have a choice of paths. He chooses both. Prayer without the support of a life of charity is hypocrisy. Our Lord told us that prayer and action must be joined when He said: "Leave thy gift at the altar, go reconcile thyself with thy brother, then offer thy sacrifice."

The contemplative religious and the dedicated layman heavily involved in temporal commitments differ only by the proportions of formal prayer and charitable activity in their lives. Contemplation and action cannot be neatly compartmentalized in the life of any Christian, whether Trappist or truck driver. All Christians are called to the love of the One God. The mode of prayer and action will differ according to the promptings of the Spirit and the circumstances of one's vocation.

Religious life through its rule, constitution, and the community's daily schedule structures prayer life for the community. It arranges for what it considers the basic minimum allotment of time for prayer for its members. Here there is the temptation to say that lay life by its nature differs on this point so radically from religious life that it is impossible for the layman to structure his prayer life. It is an easy way out to say that the world is his cloister and the busy schedule of events with their unpredictability is his breviary or incense of praise which God accepts because he makes a morning offering each day. The morning offering in the bathroom and the hasty act of contrition in the evening as the totality of one's prayer life is indeed a threadbare spiritual existence and obviously incapable of supporting a life of charity. It must be stated emphatically that every Christian worthy of the name must construct for himself a prayer life which is adequate for his life in the world and his life in God.

The center of every Catholic's prayer life should be the Mass. The Mass is the only adequate worship of Our Heavenly Father. At Mass we are not praying as individuals but as members of Christ's Mystical Body. Our hands are clasped in Christ's as He pleads with Our Heavenly Father on our behalf. In the Mass, wrote Pius XII, "Christ acts each day to save us."

The Mass has been likened to a prism which continually reflects new facets of reality to us. This is possible because of the variety of texts which we encounter in the missal as we live each year through the cycle of seasons and feasts which is called the liturgical year. "The liturgical year," wrote Pius XII, "is no cold and lifeless representation of past events, no mere historical record. Rather, it is Christ Himself, living on in His Church, and still pursuing that path of boundless mercy which, 'going about and doing good,' He began to tread during His life on earth. This He does in order to bring souls of men into contact with His mysteries, and to make them live by them. These mysteries are now constantly present and active . . . for each of them is, according to its nature and in its own way, the cause of our salvation."

In our stress over the centuries on the obligation of Sunday Mass and its sanctifying power for those physically present, we have neglected to invite people to dig for its hidden and varied treasures. Today a trickle of adult lay Catholics have become fascinated by the liturgy's lore. Through Pius Parsch's *Year of Grace* and other sources they are beginning to see new meanings in familiar phrases from the Introit or some other changeable part of the Mass.

For centuries the Mass was *the* Catholic school. It was through text, song, and action of the Mass, never in a dull, repetitive fashion, that the community taught itself. It may be that the Catholic educator's present harassment with the prohibitive cost of a complete Catholic school system will prove a blessing. It may force him to re-evaluate his question-answer, lecture-exam methods in terms of the more lively and lifegiving traditional methods of heralding the good news.

The Mass as the center of our prayer life has these four advantages: 1) it brings us to the source of divine life; 2) it offers daily short Scripture readings; 3) it relates the historic life of Christ with the actual living of the life of grace; 4) it can make the teaching of Christian doctrine a moving drama. Besides these it offers to families a backdrop for family prayer. In this country families have used effectively the Christmas creche, May altars, and pictures of the Sacred Heart as props for family prayer. Without an iconoclastic approach to the past, families with an understanding and love of the liturgy can give a family expression to the bare facts of the liturgical season explained in our daily missal. The Advent wreath, copied from German Protestants, has been the first of these customs to win wide acceptance. When many more families pioneer in family observances of liturgical and family feasts, the literature will grow and the customs will become a part of our American Catholic culture.

Liturgical and family prayer can begin with enthusiasm after exposure to their inner logic, but can pass from religious experience to lifeless rituals. The attrition of daily life can rob them of their richness. It is easy to forget that they have meaning only as long as they are an expression of a living faith in Christ. To make them meaningful and fruitful there must be daily attention given to preparing for these moments of grace. There must be a time for reflection, time to take a fresh view of our sacramental relations with Christ, time to reflect upon our human relationships in reference to Christ. I am not talking about a period of self-analysis for self-improvement, but a period of solitary prayerful reflection which brings back the glow to our faith in Christ as we participate in the sacramental life of the Church and go about our work and play. This is a period of intimacy or union with God which we call mental prayer.

The Trappist who spends four or six hours a day doing manual labor is able to live a life of uninterrupted conscious union with God because, unlike most manual laborers, he spends long periods in prayerful meditation. Because he has conditioned himself by previous periods of reflection, his mind is free as he turns his spade or digs his hoe to rest in the thought of God's presence or soar in the contemplation of God's loving concern for him. Can the layman achieve this mysticism in action? The secretary as she meticulously pencils her eyebrows and applies the delicate shadings of mascara can see in the mirror under the camouflage of cosmetics a reflection of God's image, the temple of the Holy Spirit, only if she has prepared for this moment by periods of personal prayer. The businessman who when he picks up the phone and whispers with meaning, "May God be on my lips and in my heart," is giving expression to a prayer life that demands its own time and attention. A salesman who is able to use the odd moments of the day in reflecting upon God's presence, while waiting to see a customer, acts not simply from a sudden impulse of the Holy Spirit but from long practice in the art of prayer.

Lay apostles do not form themselves by cutting down their involvement in lay life. In spite of their work away from home and at home, and a network of social and civic engagements, they must saturate their lives with prayer, making it a sweet-burning incense before God. It is true that in accepting their present life as God's will, traveling back and forth to work, attending evening meetings, doing their laundry or hair late at night, they are carrying out the injunction of St. Paul to "pray without ceasing." However, the quality of daily life as prayer will depend upon daily periods of reflection.

When can a busy layman convinced of the responsibility he has in the social order take time out each day for meditation or mental prayer? Where can he fit it into his overcrowded schedule? He may feel that he already has too many commitments. Every lay person who wants to be an effective witness for Christ or a healthy cell in the Mystical Body must grapple with these questions. He must begin with a clear and unequivocal affirmation that he must find a place in his day for an uninterrupted conversation with God. If it means setting his alarm fifteen minutes earlier, if it means giving up some activity that was previously considered necessary to his existence, this must be ruthlessly done. Without a conviction of the importance of this oasis in his daily life the layman's effectiveness as a Christian will be compromised. His busy day will be like a school child's meaningless busy-work.

When such a conviction takes shape and the commitment is made, finding the time, place, and suitable method becomes less formidable. A housewife experienced in the art of prayer writes: "The busy mother can take ten minutes while the children nap. The diapers may go unfolded but the work of the house will get done somehow; even if her own nap is shortened it's worth it. I usually snatch ten to twenty minutes in the morning right after Pete and the children leave for work and school and the baby is still asleep. The temptation is always there not to take the time. The kitchen with its undone dishes, the unmade beds, the thought of the hectic day ahead—all cry out for my immediate attention. But I find that if I take the time then, everything else does get done and my whole day gets put in perspective, too. Of course there are exceptions—a sick child, an unexpected visitor—but I do try to keep to it apart from these occasions. Pete gets up early and spends extra time at Church in the early morning and almost nothing except illness ever interferes with this precious time for him."

What does one do during this period? What is mental prayer? There are many books on the art of prayer, so I shall limit myself to a few basic observations. There is a divine simplicity of St. Teresa's description of mental prayer: "It is nothing else, in my opinion, but being on terms of friendship with God, frequently conversing with Him who, as we know, loves us." This is little different from the priest who in teaching young adults the art of prayer suggests that they begin thus: "Lord, I want to have a session with you. There are a few things I want to discuss with you."

Defining mental prayer as loving conversation with God makes it sound easy. The novice is easily deluded. Intimate conversation with a person who has been a stranger to us does not come easily, especially when this person is present to us only by faith. Fatigue comes rapidly after the initial fervor has spent itself. Then come periods of feeling spiritually sterile and being tempted to toss aside the whole business and use the time in efforts which show results. The periods of dryness or lack of intellectual and emotional response must be considered fruitful because there is present the desire for union with God which in itself is a form of union.

"Prayer will be given us," writes Father Leclercq. "It is a gift granted to each one, a personal gift, and for this reason it is considered by the ancients as something not to be organized in common, like public prayer. It comes when, how, and to the extent that the Lord wishes, but it does come. This gift on God's part, this act of consent on our part, should be prepared for by a state of prayer."

Neither the beginner nor the one skilled in the art of prayer moves from the pressures of work and traffic jams, from diapers and dishes, to a loving consideration of the Trinity, without a bridge that connects these two worlds. Spiritual reading, whether public, as in the liturgy, or private has always served this purpose. The purpose of spiritual reading is to prepare us for, to provoke, or to stimulate a personal contact with God. It leads us to the moment when we put the reading aside, close our eyes, and open ourselves to God. It is the pump primer for personal prayer.

In the early Church there was only one book, the Bible. Today there are libraries of books related to God's revelation of Himself. If a book is to be judged as spiritual reading it should lead us back to the Bible as our primary source of Christian wisdom or should help us to apply God's word as found in the Bible to the contemporary scene. Books dealing with our relationship to God must be judged not only on their orthodoxy but on our felt needs at the moment.

One advantage of a liturgical orientation for one's prayer life is that the missal provides a steady diet of rich spiritual food. The Scripture lessons of each day's Mass offer phrases, sentences, and longer passages that a person can chew on during his period of mental prayer. The resurgence of Bible studies has brought with it more readable and less expensive paperback translations of the books of the Bible, with commentaries. The layman who chooses the commuter train for his period of mental prayer will find that the pocketbook edition of the New Testament has obvious advantages. In spiritual reading which we combine or relate with mental prayer we should be reluctant to stray very far from God's writings about Himself.

If great novelists such as Tolstoy, Dostoevski, or Mauriac evoke in us an abiding compassion, do they not offer us a fitting prelude to communion with God and deserve the classification of religious literature or spiritual reading? The morning paper provides material for seeing in human events the agony of the Mystical Body as it fills up "those things which are wanting in the Body of Christ." The plight of the migrant worker, of peasant in Vietnam or China, of the Negro in our own South —or North—these and others can spark us to prayer. But the constant refrain of our message is that the Bible is our basic text. We are more likely by reading widely to develop our sensitivities and compassion and relate them to Christ if the bedrock of our reading and reflection is the unadulterated word of God.

Just as the worker feels the need of long holiday week ends and an annual vacation wherein he can get a better perspective on his life and refresh himself, so the Christian needs equivalent periods for more lengthy reflection. The Church structures such periods. The parish mission has been until recently the only widely used form. Parochial and extra-parochial groups increasingly offer days of recollection to their membership. While these are generally beneficial, often the period of time is so telescoped that the periods of silence are too short for lengthy reflection. Lay people, too, are critical of the talks, not in the sense of a lack of sympathy for and appreciation of the priest's efforts, but they would like to know in advance if the speaker is going to challenge them sufficiently and stir them from their present spiritual status to warrant hiring a baby sitter and depriving their family of their presence. Many, without cynicism, express their boredom with the phrase, "pre-Mystical Body teaching," and recognize the patronizing appeal to the minimum that they are receiving. This is not a lack of faith in the ministry of the Word but realism about the economy of time and the most effective means of receiving God's Word.

Not all lay people leave completely to chance the finding of time for lengthy periods of reflection. Many are finding ways to spend a week end a year in prayerful silence. The growth in retreat houses in this country is nothing less than phenomenal. A retreat, in contrast to a day or evening of recollection, puts emphasis on an atmosphere of silence and the creative power of well-used leisure time, rather than on the eloquence of the retreat master. Traditionally, retreats have been segregated by sexes. Presently the number of retreats for married couples and families is steadily increasing.

For those to whom a retreat away from home would be a practical impossibility, a housewife makes the following suggestion: "I'm on a three-day retreat right here at home. I go to morning Mass while Mike gets the children up and gives the baby his bottle. Then the older children help him get breakfast. I'm home from Mass by the time he leaves for work and the older children go to school. When the little ones go out to play

I do some spiritual reading, then start the housework. After lunch when the babies are napping, I have time to read some more and sometimes say the rosary. In the evening Mike and the older children put the babies to bed while I go into the bedroom, close the door, and read some more."

While the mature Christian realizes that flexibility and adaptability are cornerstones for apostolic lay life, he knows, too, that he cannot be rudderless and let himself be completely ruled by the fury of the winds and the waves. He learns to prize, like the true monk does his cell, an occasional evening spent at home with his own thoughts. It may be late in the evening when, with a book in hand, he permits his mind and heart to ponder the eternal verities which his reading evokes. The businessman who has a long trip to make by car may choose to turn off the radio and reflect on his latest Bible reading or on a human relationship he has taken for granted. These lengthy periods of solitude are necessary for perspective. They must be hewed out of a busy life. The American Catholic layman can witness to his nervous country that contemplation is not a spiritual luxury.

XIII

MYSTICISM IN ACTION

The life of Christ offers the psychology class or the instructor in the dynamics of human behavior a book on the art of human persuasion. While He was resting at the well of Jacob a sinful Samaritan woman came to draw water. He approached her by asking her to draw Him some water. The greatest gift we can confer upon a person is to give him the opportunity of helping others. The woman responded to Jesus' confidence in her, and the conversation went from well water to living water and finally to her sinfulness. When she discovered that she was accepted in spite of her sinfulness, she became an apostle and heralded His name and deeds to the townsfolk.

Although we know little about Simon of Cyrene, the legend is that, after his initial reluctance to carry the Cross with Christ, he joyfully shared with Christ its weight and the insults of the crowd. When our Lord was picking his first apostles, He did not pass out brochures on apostolic careers or give speeches on the urgency of the apostolate. He simply gave an invitation to come and experience living with Him: "Come and see."

The Good Samaritan story ends with an appeal to action or service. This is the acid test of the Christian. At the Last Supper our Lord insisted over the protest of Peter on washing the feet of the Apostles. Words are words and are easily forgotten. Deeds have a substance to them that are not dispersed like random thoughts. The touch of Christ's hands in washing their dirty and calloused feet would be the key for the Apostles that would unlock the meaning of the discourse He made for them at the Last Supper, which declared that the mark of Christians would be their love one for another. After the Resurrection Christ confirmed His teachings and actions by the fish-fry He prepared for the Apostles after their night of labor at sea.

Everyone subscribes to love as the basis of human relations but when it comes to finding its expression in the multiple and intricate human relations of every day, we need the emotional experience of having loved or been loved the previous day. Love comes from experience, not study. Meditation on love is not love but a preparation for the experience of love.

Our Lord did not teach His disciples the art of praying until they were well along with their apostolic training. In fact, their request, not our Lord's initiative, brought them instruction in the art of prayer. The Our Father was given to us at their request. Our Lord's disciples had their first closed retreat *after* a missionary journey. Prayer is more meaningful when we have had an encounter which reveals our confusions and mixed emotions. We are more willing and able to engage in combat with ourselves after we experience failure and self-exposure to our own weakness.

Writers and preachers on prayer relate the dire consequences of the activist who is so caught up in his "good works" that he forgets that the intended action be performed "through Him, with Him, and in Him." How seldom do we hear the same people admonish those who give themselves to long prayers and much fasting but studiously refrain from becoming involved in the stresses and strains, the groans and the anguish of the strivings of the people of our times, whether they be living in the same block or the next block, the same nation or another continent.

Our Lord's compassion for the prostitutes and adulterers stands in sharp contrast with His treatment of the stiff-necked Pharisees. In our Lord's parable the Pharisee, by his own declaration, was a man of prayer and fasting. Nowhere else in the Gospel is there an example of greater invective by our Lord than in His dealing with these men of prayer. "Stiffnecked," "brood of vipers," and "whitened sepulchers" are not terms of endearment. If we permit ourselves to become involved in the anxieties of our fellow men, our sleep may be disturbed but our personalities will become transformed by compassion. Prayer plus involvement adds up to compassion. Prayer without active concern for our neighbor makes us righteous, unlovable Pharisees, unfit for the Kingdom.

How do we form or shape Catholics for Christian witness in this world? How do we prepare lay people for making a total commitment to Christ within the present context of their lives? There seem to be two approaches within the stream of American Catholicism. The traditional and entrenched view sees it as a vast effort in instruction on the major tenets of our faith with a view to a faithful observance of the Mass, marriage laws, and dietary obligations. There is much to be said for this emphasis. It has aided the immigrant flock to cleave to its religious and national identity in hostile or at least new surroundings. It has built massive Catholic institutions, staffed schools with countless consecrated religious men and women. A series of sociological studies verify the fact that the statistical religious observance of Catholics has not significantly suffered from the pressures of urban life, the pull of secularism, and the waning of moral standards.

There is another view, although with less acceptance and respectability, which seems to me to be closer to our Lord's way of training people. It does not believe that the imparting of religious information about the Church and the measurable observance of its precepts is the final goal of the Christian or the Church or the best way to train people for Christian responsibility in this world. It holds that instruction must be more than the mere imparting of information about the Church, that it must be orientated toward a vital adhesion to the Risen Christ as our Savior. It holds that every human effort should be extended to make each religious service or observance an encounter with God — what, in modern literature, is called a religious experience. In the field of catechetics this view is known as the kerygmatic revival, and in Church prayer and worship as the liturgical apostolate.

In terms of actual training, as opposed to formal teaching, the Catholic Action methods of the past quarter century closely resemble our Lord's dealings with His Apostles. Pope John in *Mater et Magistra* has canonized these methods and approach, introduced into the Church at the historic meeting of Canon Cardijn and Pius XI in 1925. It was the meeting of a pope who had intense convictions about training lay people in a realistic way for the apostolate of the Church and a pioneering youth leader who had worked out a method but lacked the approval of his bishop. Cardijn differed from the great youth leaders of his day by his belief that the seeds of any reform movement lie within the group to be reformed. It was not simply a question of legislation against cruel working conditions or their amelioration by the paternalism of the mighty. Nor did Cardijn think that a priest-worker movement was the answer. The young people must believe in themselves and address themselves to their own problems. They must see in themselves and their fellow workers the image of God. He taught young people to take up their Cross and follow Jesus in His sufferings. He was teaching a modern way of the Cross built on joyous service and heroic suffering. This type of Catholic lay movement, which can no longer be restricted to specialized Catholic Action, is a way of finding and growing in Christ through confrontation with real life. It is learning Christ through the acceptance of responsibility for our brothers in need. It is the mystical experience of Christ as we find Him in our homes, and places of work and play.

Pope John, writing in *Mater et Magistra* with the conviction of Cardijn and the authority of the papal office, states: "Education to act in a Christian manner in economic and social matters will hardly succeed, in our opinion, unless those being educated play an active role in their own formation, and unless formal instruction is supplemented by activity undertaken for the sake of gaining experience." He repeats the Cardijn formula for the formation of modern lay Christians: "In reducing social principles and directives in practice, one usually goes through three stages: reviewing the actual situation, judging it in the light of these principles and directives, and deciding what can and should be done to apply these traditional norms to the extent that the situation will permit. These three stages are usually expressed in three terms: observe, judge, act."

In *Mater et Magistra* Pope John writes for the universal Church. He does not plead the cause of a particular organization. He states principles which must be applied differently to countries, times, and groups. With all these qualifications there is no question with him of the relationship of instruction and action. It is succinct: "From instruction and education one must pass to action."

In our age of discussion, study groups and discussion clubs have proliferated in Catholic circles. The test of the discussion club as opposed to the action group is whether the study group is willing to confront issues which strike at the sensitivities of the group and expose the individual prejudices of the members. The test is whether the study group will dig sufficiently deep to destroy its own clichés. Study must precede action if we are dealing with a complex social problem. Many action groups work at cross-purposes with the Church because of their moral and intellectual failure to find out what the Church's scholars and practitioners are writing and saying on contemporary problems. Cardinal Saliège speaks forthrightly on the characteristic weakness of both study and action groups:

> I have known lay apostolate groups which are closed sections, study groups, friendly gatherings, in which the participants split hairs four ways, carry on endless discussions on nothing, and drain their minds and hearts dry. They beat around the bush; they never go to the center of things. They admire each other and do nothing. They bore each other methodically. They fear the world of time, they are afraid they may slip into it. They have no spirit, they have no courage, they have no daring. Inevitably, people who are worth anything stay away

from such groups. The lay apostolate will not attract worthwhile human beings unless it is engaged with the human, and therefore, with the things of time.

More than ever the current of history is toward action, toward wholehearted action, and not toward talk—talk which is childish, a niggling inanity alongside the profound transformation for which the world is waiting. There are methods for training altar boys. These methods are not suited to lay apostles, because the aim of the lay apostolate is not to form altar boys. Its aim is to bend social pressure in the direction of life. In taking flesh, the lay apostolate comes out of its dream and gets into reality, into the social, the material, the economic, and the temporal. It acts.

Such words as encounter, engagement, dialogue, involvement, and confrontation have punctuated this book, and this chapter in particular. They suggest a face-to-face meeting with one's true self, another person, an unpleasant truth, or a social fact. They call for a facing-up to reality rather than an ostrichlike avoidance of it. Yet there are many races, national groups, and social situations we cannot encounter because of the social and racial stratification of society. We seldom have a face-to-face encounter with a member of a racial minority because of our segregated urban areas. We seldom meet foreign visitors or students because their paths never cross ours. We may have no experiential awareness of many social problems which are festering wounds on the social body of which the Mystical Christ is formed. We may feel like the man in the Gospel with the withered limbs who had no one to move him to the water that he might be cured.

The kind of encounters mentioned above are almost impossible without organization. Such organization is being provided in the field of race relations by Chicago's Friendship House, which in a growing number of cities, is sponsoring meetings between white and Negro families in each other's homes, where people can talk out their hopes and fears, their love and hate. In large cities where there are college campuses, foreign-visitor and foreign-student committees have been organized to make contacts between local families and the visitors or students for tours of the city, picnics, international nights, and the hospitality of family gatherings. The effect upon the American family involved in such a project is to know Nigeria, not as a nation in a politically tense part of the world whose friendship must be won solely with tax dollars, but as the nation of the charming Nigerian, Charles, who graced their table last Easter.

The American Peace Corps is designed to train generous young Americans for a limited period of service in a foreign land. It has a twofold purpose: 1) to give technical assistance to nations which seek this kind of help; 2) to create good will abroad for the United States. There is a little-mentioned side effect which may as the decades go on be the most significant contribution of the Peace Corps to the world. After a few years these young men and women will return to civilian life in their local communities. The effect which their stint in a foreign land will have upon their families and local communities may well result in a revolution in international understanding and cooperation on a grass-roots level.

In Minneapolis the Catholic Youth Center has started its own peace corps for high-school students. One of the basic tenets of their "Contact" program is that the formation of the Christian must be through an encounter wherein he finds Christ in the needs of others and ministers to Him. It is more than a textbook or discussion operation. It demands sacrifice and violence to one's anti-Christian feelings.

For example, an all-day study day brought out two hundred students on a Sunday for an intense day of training. Following a lecture on the Mystical Body, each student, as part of a highly organized plan, knocked on doors in an area thirty blocks square, asking for canned goods to help feed the derelicts at the House of Charity in the center of the city. They collected 1,182 cans of food, $5, two bananas, two packages of powdered ice cream, and three cans of cat food. It was an experience in living Christianity which was capable of giving a new dimension to their classroom concept of Christ.

Young people look forward to leaving their books and teachers for a summer of work and play and the possible luxury of a prolonged trip to a distant recreation center. The Minneapolis Contact Peace Corps offers to high-school students "an exciting summer . . . full of opportunities, travel, thought, and experience." They offer twenty-five possibilities for teams of volunteers. Students can go in groups to San Jose, California, to assist groups serving migrant workers; they can take part in established religious instruction and art and craft programs for children in Lafayette, Louisiana; or they can assist at interracial centers in Chicago or Brooklyn.

All twenty-five projects demand special training courses, besides a fund-raising program, before the group boards its bus or train for its engagement with Christ in the needy. It is the devout prayer of the Contact Corps staff that after a team has traveled a thousand miles and had an exciting adventure in charity, they will more easily find Christ in their parents, their teachers, and their classmates. In place of a sun tan and detailed accounts of the exciting foods in the Duncan Hines-approved restaurants, they can bring back to their social science classes an existential awareness of Christian responsibility in the world in which we live.

On an open-end TV student discussion program, Miss Shelby Hickey of Smith College made some profound observations about formation through action. She expressed her desire to take part in direct social action but also her conflicting desire to spend more time studying, not for better grades, but for a deeper comprehension of the issues involved in the causes for which students demonstrate.

Some students, she explained, are led from demonstrations to a more meaningful intellectual life. The picket line arouses their intellectual curiosity. Their academic work can be more fruitful because of the emotional experience of engaging in front-line combat for social justice. The student, however, who spends all her time crusading may never receive an education and because of her lack of intellectual depth may make her social action merely destructive or at best a futile protest for protest's sake. Action and learning should be complementary and feed upon each other. Each person must work out his own mixture according to his lights and talents.

In this country the Church has put practically all its eggs in the educational basket. This is why the federal aid to education issue looms so large in Catholic circles. Catholic education has given two characteristics to the American Church for which it is known around the world, namely, observance of Church law and a high degree of religious literacy. Catholic education never set out to form lay apostles and get total commitment to Christ from its graduates. It sought to protect them from encounter with the world. This is not meant as an adverse criticism of Catholic education. Commitment to anything is not a textbook affair. It is as much or more an emotional or volitional response than an intellectual one.

Rattling off catechism answers is one thing; laying down one's life day by day for Christ is another. Commitment to Christ means that laymen in every walk of life must take seriously Christ's call to "sell what thou hast, give to the poor, and come follow Me." It does not mean that the layman must sell his suburban home and move to the slums, but that he must live his life with the same dedication and consecration which the Apostles had. He cannot let middle-class living become a split-level trap.

How do we get this kind of commitment from lay people? The Catholic Worker and interracial centers of the thirties and forties offered the best example. Instead of being greeted with a lecture series on the Mystical Body, people were given a paring knife and a sack of potatoes, or a scrubbing brush they could use to clean a smelly walk-up Harlem apartment. If the person met the challenge, he would experience the doctrine of the Mystical Body as the Apostles did, rather than as a memory exercise in a Catholic classroom. The commitment came from an actual encounter with Christ. The person knew Christ rather than knew about Him. He met Him and fed Him and served Him in every need that was apparent.

The era of store-front Christianity seems far removed from our better organized apostolic organizations and movements. Nevertheless the job remains for all groups to help their members face the crisis of Christianity in their own lives. The Catholic organization which wishes to train its members for a modern apostolate must continually plunge people into crisis. It must shock them with the words of our Lord. It must prod them, upset them, disturb them. There is no point in engaging people in academic debate. People too often use dialogue for subterfuge and rationalization. To advocate such a shock approach is not to be anti-intellectual, but is simply to recognize the problem of getting people to shake off their lethargy. How else can comfortable middle-class people, who diet on Martinis and Metrecal, be confronted with a challenge to a radical living of the Gospel?

Why is the early Church the model for all the centuries of Christianity? The early Christians stuck their necks out in a very literal fashion. These were the centuries of mass martyrdom, not cozy Christianity. Today Catholic laymen must be plunged into situations where they will be forced to choose or reject Christ. We must remember that in the age of martyrdom there were Christians who failed to embrace martyrdom and capitulated. It was not an age of caution or an age of weak-kneed prudence. Christians were not overprotected then; they were given a chance to fail Christ. Without this chance to reject Him there can be no loving embrace of Him.

Laymen in our metropolitan areas should be glad to receive the hisses and boos of their neighbors when they welcome a Negro family into their neighborhood. Catholic students everywhere in the country should be encouraged to take part in Gandhi type sit-in demonstrations protesting injustice. This kind of thing disturbs family relationships, but our Lord has told us to expect this. He has encouraged us to violence. He has told us that households will be divided because of Him.

A priest in Oklahoma City was arrested for taking part in a sit-in. His bishop's statement in his defense was carefully and poignantly worded. He said that bearing witness against social injustices was ordinarily the task of the layman, but because the laity had failed one of his priests had rightly stepped into the breach. The priest did not crowd any lay people out of the police wagon.

What are we doing as a result of all we have read, seen, and heard about the Congo, Cuba, and Laos? Are we content to bewail the aggressiveness of the Communists or be Monday-morning quarterbacks for the White House and State Department moves? What did we do for the babies with bloated bellies in the Congo? What interest did we take in the Cuban refugees in Florida? What have we done for the lay missions of the type Tom Dooley started in Laos?

In our newspaper reading we must learn to see Christ in His agony, not simply the effect of the news on the stock market. For the love of Christ we must seek out foreign students and visitors to our area and break bread with them, not simply for better world relations but because Christ identifies Himself with the stranger. "I was a stranger and you took Me in."

Commitment to Christ simply means commitment to our needy neighbor regardless of where he may be, what the color of his skin may be, what religious group he may belong to. The crisis of the Church in America is not one of formal education but of commitment.

XIV

FORMING THE CATHOLIC CONSCIENCE

It is obvious that the American Catholic conscience has huge gaps. It has an individualistic rather than a social orientation. It is concerned with individual perfection apart from the social context of our human encounters. It is concerned with self-improvement almost to the exclusion of the improvement of the social institutions which shape the lives and mores of our people. It is ostrichlike in its approach to the world. In our efforts to keep ourselves unspotted there is almost a contempt for the legitimate strivings of mankind. One would think that the social order was irrelevant to the Christian, as though it was something other than the interaction of people in their struggle towards genuine human goals. The individualism of the old morality is as dead as colonialism and as bankrupt as the Confederate government.

One notable exception must be made to this indictment of the American Catholic conscience. It is in the area of family life. Catholic morality holds doggedly, against overwhelming public opinion, to the indissolubility of the marriage bond and the wrongness of artificial birth control. However the gap between the proclamation and the practice of family morality leaves much to be desired. Too little attention is given to what creates the gap. Catholic family morality is not sufficiently related to the pressures for higher status, more education, employment, housing, and medical care. Even in their own fortress of family morality Catholics need to widen the horizons of their social conscience.

When people are lined up outside a confessional on a Christmas Eve or a Saturday afternoon, on what points are they examining their consciences? This probing implies some kind of an objective standard by which one can judge. We would like to think that there is such a reality as the Christian conscience, that is, a consensus of Christians in a particular culture as to what is right and wrong in all major aspects of human behavior. When an employer who refuses to bargain fairly with his employees, or an employee who extends coffee breaks fifteen minutes or a half hour a day, confesses only sins of impurity, anger, missing meal-prayers, and swearing, we would say that he has a seventh-grade code of morality and is thus morally retarded. When it never occurs to a mother in going to confession that she failed to prepare herself for an election by taking an interest in the issues of the campaign or that she did not encourage her children's interest in their secular studies, we conclude that her view of Christianity is severely restricted and her conscience has vast underdeveloped areas. It may well be that she was so much concerned with not committing sins of birth control and cutting down on petty gossip that she had no mental or moral energy for wider human or social concerns.

The typical parish mission shows our limited and narrow approach to morality. The great sins treated are those opposed to marriage. The abuse of sex, nagging, and laxity in parental supervision head the list. How often is charity spelled out in terms of the racial conflict around us and our responsibilities to our brethren in the emerging African nations? A discerning wife once remarked to me that she did not think it worthwhile to hire a baby sitter to care for her brood while she went to a mission to be lectured on abortion and birth control. The same woman would gladly ring doorbells to get people out to a mission if she knew that the preacher would effectively deal with the virtue of charity in a way that related it to the realities of her life.

After centuries of individualism the training of a conscience that is sensitive to the responsibilities of our times is a task of no mean proportions. It must be undertaken on two levels: The acceptance of principles and the applications of these principles to particular situations. From Pope Leo's *Rerum Novarum* in 1891 to Pope John's *Mater et Magistra* in 1961, we have had a steady stream of papal pronouncements which deal with basic moral principles in the social order. The Catholic press, with notable exceptions, and Catholic schools, to a limited degree, have expounded the practical applications of the Church's social teaching. Yet our traditional methods of pen, pulpit, and classroom have not formed our people in such a way that the image of the American Catholic is that of a person with a social conscience. We have yet to exploit sufficiently methods of educating the Catholic conscience in a morality or outlook that embraces the concerns of Christ outside the self-centered view of the individual Christian.

The conscience is trained through being focussed on life situations, as a soldier is trained through combat. Every age has a particular social problem which serves as a catalyst to focus the nation's and the individual's struggle of conscience. Since the Supreme Court decision on school integration, in 1954, the race problem has been the proving ground for American Christianity. The Catholic conscience must squarely face the race issue.

For generations our Catholic and Protestant brethren in the South have been brought up in religious homes, studied in Church-related segregated schools, and worshiped in Jim Crow churches. Now they rebel when they are told that segregation is sinful. Their violent emotional reactions testify to their feelings on being told in adult life that the formula for their examination of conscience was defective. They take it as an indictment of their religious and loving parents, their devoted school teachers, and the preachers who omitted the subject of race from their inspiring example, admonitions, and sermons on Christian love.

In northern cities, from pulpits, textbooks, and newspapers consciences are adequately formed to accept the theoretical proposition that all men are equal, that human rights are not to be denied to anyone because of race, creed, color, or place of national origin. But how do we explain the kind of incident symbolized by Deerfield? Deerfield, Illinois, is the all-white community which voted two-to-one to condemn for public purposes the property of a developer who was going to sell to Negro buyers. *But Not Next Door* (Ivan Oblensky, Inc.), a study of the Deerfield scandal, catches the mental anguish of people who must rationalize the decisions of their troubled consciences: "We're not bigots. We don't go around calling people names. And I don't think we want to deny Negroes or anybody else the right to decent homes, just as good as ours. But not next door."

Deerfield stands for the conscience which is correctly formed intellectually but is unable or unwilling to apply principles to a concrete set of circumstances. There is a failure in the virtue of prudence or the art of practical judgment. The *But Not Next Door* mentality reveals another aspect of the formation of conscience. Overzealous partisans of Catholic education give the impression that all a Catholic needs to do to form a Catholic conscience is to sit in a Catholic classroom, study from Catholic textbooks, and pass exams by Catholic teachers. This is an American version of the Gnostic heresy, which equates knowledge with virtue.

Through Catholic education we teach people the basic truths and precepts of the Church. We have been relatively successful in our heroic efforts to impart this religious information. Through home and parochial school efforts we have been successful in training young people to form habits of Catholic practice such as Sunday Mass, monthly confession, meatless Fridays, and, for a growing number, daily Mass during Lent and Communion at each Mass in which they participate. These are positive gains. However, if they are considered as a total formation for living a Christian life they are hopelessly inadequate in our dynamic and pluralistic society.

What is needed is not less Catholic education but an entirely new concept of Christian formation. Forming consciences by rote, by memorized formulas, is not enough. The training of the Christian can only be done by a continual process of re-evaluation of life situations. Since each person cannot have his own moral theologian to consult a dozen times a day, the practical way seems to be a method where the group whose members all face similar situations helps form a consensus based on the facts of experience and the teachings of Christ and the Church. It seems that the best results come from freewheeling discussions with the help of experts, whether they are clerical or lay.

Publishing a code of conduct for every area of lay life might seem an easier solution and save the endless rounds of discussion which leave so many loose ends untied. If the Catholic moralist were able to codify his opinions on every subject relevant to lay life and then see that they were distributed to every home, the millennium in Catholic morality would not have been reached. How would the individual be sure he was applying the rules correctly? He would argue that the moralist was writing for someone with circumstances different from his. And what would he do while waiting for the code to be published, or revised to include new problems?

During the past decade our large cities have produced codes for Catholic teen-age conduct. The strength of this type of code is that it has been born out of discussion between parents, children, and priests. Each has considered the others' viewpoints and a broad consensus is achieved before the code is promulgated. This approach allows for the diversity of cultural patterns, takes into account the group pressures which militate against compliance, and allows for individual freedom. Unquestionably the greatest benefit of the code accrues to those who enter into the preliminary discussions prior to its formulation. The participants receive a practical education in Christian morality and the forming of a Christian conscience in this narrow area of life.

At an early Catholic Action meeting in this country a young man out of school held an audience of priests spellbound. He told them plainly that the answers to the problems of modern life were not to be found in their moral theology books. "Books," he said, "are written about problems that are already solved." He was pleading with them to deal with contemporary problems which are at their backdoor and which defy the solutions of authors who live in an academic world.

In effect he was telling them that their parishioners are living in a dynamic society where circumstances are always changing and new situations arising, so that lay people must be in a sense their own guides or theologians. They must have the facility, promptness, and courage to make their own decisions and accept responsibility for them. They must be able to trust their own decision-making ability and act on it.

The lay Christian cannot be always sure of himself. What he does is to make a cultural approximation of the Christian thing to do, given the situation and the necessity to act. The fact that he can never be sure that he acted prudently does not deter him. He humbly accepts this built-in insecurity as the inevitable condition of a layman in a pluralistic society. Practice in decision-making ordinarily improves the quality of the decisions and ultimately narrows the margin of error.

In our society the group-discussion method offers invaluable help in the formation of conscience. If the group is composed of people who face similar problems in the world, they are able to compare notes. Occasionally the sum of knowledge will be the sum of zeros, when the members of the group are totally lacking in insight or their minds are completely closed. If, on the contrary, there are members of the group who do some reading, are seriously struggling with the problem discussed, have a large view of the Christian's total responsibility, each member of the group can refine his thinking on the subject. The collective judgment of the group will very likely epitomize mature Christian wisdom from which a practical course can be taken by each member of the group.

Recently a group of Chicago businessmen became concerned about how they were handling their expense accounts. They sought out a priest who was a specialist in the field of social action and public morality. He told them that he would be glad to sit in on a discussion of the matter with them. He would listen while they discussed. At the end of the meeting the priest expressed the feeling of inadequacy he had as the discussion progressed. He was aware as were the other members of the group of the general moral principles about the responsibility of the individual to himself and his family, to his employer and the common good, but he did not work for a corporation where the rules of the company and the accepted practice were at variance. No one left the meeting with precise rules on expense accounts. However, through the exchange, each participant was better able to put his own situation in focus and to feel more secure in his day-to-day solutions.

I began this chapter questioning the maturity of the social conscience of the lay Catholic who stands in line for confession on Saturday afternoon. The major emphasis of the discussion was placed on the confrontation of the layman with life situations. Another element in the formation of a mature conscience is in a faithful daily examination of conscience. If a person goes to confession annually, he will likely only remember the most serious transgressions against his code of sexual morality and the precepts of the Church. If he goes monthly, his categories of sin will likely be more numerous and more specific. If he goes biweekly, he may find that he is a greater sinner than if he went bimonthly. Since he cannot receive the sacrament of Penance daily, the daily examination of conscience can be not only a preparation for his biweekly or monthly confession but it can be a method of developing a more sensitive conscience.

How does one pursue this daily examination of conscience? Does he run through the Ten Commandments to recall whom he killed, what he stole, and how many lies he told? We might take a clue from our Lord's farewell address at the Last Supper.

He gave charity, or love, primacy by referring to it as *His* commandment, a *new* commandment, and designating it as the mark of the Christian. "By this shall all men know that you are My disciples...."

While it is true that there is a long category of Christian virtues, they can all be viewed from the perspective of love without destroying them. St. Paul in 1 Corinthians 13, spells out charity's primacy. Because we make charity the overruling virtue, justice is not neglected. For example, if an employer loves his employees, he will not only listen to the problems of each, but he will pay them a wage that is due to them in justice and see that the conditions of work are in keeping with their dignity as sons of God. The employee in turn will show his Christian love to his employer not only by his courtesy, his respect for authority, and his efforts to understand the pressures on the employer, but by fulfilling to the letter the demands of the work contract.

To be meaningful, an examination of conscience must get down to particulars. Each person must make his own detailed listing. The following examination of offenses against charity is excerpted from a longer one covering a wider field (taken from the Fall, 1957, issue of *Cross Currents*). It is offered as a model. Each of us must compose his own.

In regard to others, have I—
   failed to take a passionate stand for the betterment of all the human race?
   considered no one but myself?
   lacked initiative in work for the common good?
   never felt real anguish for the misery of others?
   passed by, indifferent to others' troubles?
   had habitual contempt for others: less educated people, people of different racial, national or economic groups?
   in any way stifled the personal development of another?
   sought to be respected without respecting others?
   often kept others waiting?
   forgotten or not kept a date?
   not kept my promises or engagements?
   been difficult for others to reach, and too busy simply to put myself at their disposal?

not paid entire attention to a person speaking to me?
talked too much of myself, and not given others a chance
   to express themselves?
failed to try to understand others?
been too selfish, or concerned with popular opinion, to do
   a favor?
failed to do all I can to make myself fit for greater service?
out of selfishness or pride, expected to be served?
been able but neglected to lessen someone's distress?
failed to help a person in danger?
seen only those whose friendship might prove profitable?
abandoned my friends in their difficulties?
done harm, by remarks (false or true) that blackened
   others' characters; or done this simply by excessive chatter?
betrayed a trust; violated a confidence; involved myself
   in others' affairs by indiscreet words or attitudes?
"pulverized" my opponents?

XV

GROUP SUPPORT

Loneliness is not a new development in American life. James McBride Dabbs sees it even in the faces of the pioneers. "These folks were lonely, I think, because in their continual moving they left so many things behind, they tended increasingly to keep themselves from being involved in things, from loving them, and were satisfied merely to use them. But to refuse to be involved is almost by definition to be lonely."

Loneliness in America has taken a new twist. The offspring of the lonely pioneer has moved to our urban areas. Through mass activities he simulates a togetherness described in the graphic title, *The Lonely Crowd*. Huddled in crowds, modern men "lead lives of quiet desperation." They preserve their loneliness by refusing to become involved in work, play, or life any more than is necessary for survival. They learn how to protect themselves both from their own emotions and the feelings and anxieties of others. To permit exposure to another as a human being is foolishly "sticking out one's neck" or not "playing it cool." The lonely person substitutes for a genuine human encounter the shallow waters of shared likes and dislikes concerning things that do not touch the core of his being. The result is the huddling together of people obsessed with neurotic fears. The people who are not involved in a "cause" live in what amount to cell blocks in urban prisons.

Young people look to marriage as a way of overcoming their loneliness, isolation, or despair. This most intimate form of human community or involvement holds out the promise of a mutual and all-inclusive support against the claws of a rapacious world and the demonic fears that drive people to antisocial forms of escape. The evidence that marriage does not automatically fulfill this promise needs no proof.

Marriage failures are attributed to lack of maturity. This explanation is inadequate because it does not take into account the hostility of the American way of life to marriage as an institution. In a patriarchal society the clan offered support not only to young married people but to all members of the family. There was a wide assortment of relationships to give this intimate assistance in adjusting to each new phase of life. The village and parish which had the same boundaries and formed a single community offered the couple multiple emotional supports and acceptance. Ideally each partner had a sense of belonging and recognition, as a person, in the community. The clan, the village, and the parish interlocked to form a single "family."

Our modern industrial life has fractured the extended family by making the political community an anonymous organization. The parish has become a sacramental supermarket. The school and office or factory are places where human worth is evaluated by marks and units of production. The demands of school, work, and social life scatter the family by high-speed transportation devices over a metropolitan area that embraces millions of people. Under such severe pressures family ties barely hold together by thin, frayed threads. Insecure young people who look to marriage to give them security are unrealistic in their demands upon our twentieth-century patterns of family life.

Some months ago I watched a TV program which dramatized an experiment of the Navy in dealing with deeply disturbed psychological casualties of the Korean War. The group spanned the extremes from the man staring into space to the powerful sergeant seeking to give physical expression to his hostility. A psychiatrist told the men that he would meet them each morning as a group and that they could talk about anything they desired, without fear of reprisals by the authorities. After a few meetings in which they tested the psychiatrist's promise of acceptance of themselves, they began to express feelings which they had been previously unwilling to admit to themselves. It occurred to me as I watched the show that this was merely an exaggerated dramatization of a basic need of all of us. All through life we feel the need for the kind of therapy which comes from a healthy friendship group. When the group gives acceptance and understanding to each of its members, each receives a fresh grant of freedom and the possibility of intellectual, emotional, and spiritual growth. Freedom is found not in escape from people but in opening our true selves to others.

With the disappearance of the old style family grouping, there is emerging a new form of "family" life or Christian community which is rich in possibilities. These new groupings fulfill the needs of intimate and meaningful friendships and a common commitment to a lay apostolic way of life. They are an admission that the single Catholic family or the single Christian is severely limited in built-in resources. Persons in these situations do not have sufficient supports for spiritual growth as members of a family, as intelligent citizens of this world, or as apostolically orientated members of the Church.

The members of the new style Catholic "family" are united not by the blood of kin but by the blood of Christ which they share through a common faith. They are not bound together simply as members of a particular parish or neighborhood but through a common interest that gets to the core of their existence and has vital meanings in the lives of each of them. The groupings are less formal, smaller, and more intimate than the typical tightly-structured large membership Catholic organization. The ties with the parish or diocese will vary with the specific object of the group and its particular needs.

Some of these groups will be local, small-group units of wider apostolic movements. Others will be spontaneous outgrowths of such movements which are not officially linked to the Church and more closely resemble a loosely organized friendship group. Still others could hardly be called groups but rather are a network of friendships which are based on a sharing of certain values. These friendships may come into being by chance acquaintance or from previous associations with movements or projects.

Moralists, preachers, and educators are gradually becoming aware of the psychological and social barriers which stand between intellectual assent to their pronouncements and translation of them into the context of daily life. The trained counselor deals with this phenomenon every day. The client relates his feelings and his inability to deal with a situation. The counselor by skilled listening and questions helps the client to objectify his emotions, to see more clearly the blocks that are impeding constructive action. By his empathy the counselor is giving the client the support needed to come to grips with the situation in its elementary dimensions. Increasingly we are becoming aware of the potential of the group to give this kind of support to its members.

The apostolic friendship group offers to its members a built-in counseling service. At meetings people feel free to explore their feelings or give support to feelings expressed by others. Hostile and irrational feelings can be easily dissipated by the simple admission of possessing them to a sympathetic group. When we find acceptance in the presence of friends, we receive the courage to face our fears and the daring to give more of ourselves to others.

This support begins at meetings where convictions are shared and minds explored, but the full expression develops outside of the meetings in the context of daily life. The following telephone conversation illustrates a simple experience which when repeated daily in varied situations makes possible the living of the kind of life one would like to live but ordinarily finds impossible because of the social pressures in which he finds himself enmeshed.

Helen: "I just received a letter asking me to enroll my seventh-grader in the Belle Air Charm School." Kathy: "Oh, I received one, come to think of it. I threw it in the wastebasket." Helen: "Thanks so much, Kathy. You are always so helpful. I wanted someone to tell me I was doing the right thing in throwing mine away." The case was closed. If this type of interaction among parents in a neighborhood was repeated hundreds of times a day, a distinct family-life culture would evolve that would be a pattern for urban mid-century America.

Many people have made retreats at which daily Mass, spiritual reading, and mental prayer were presented in most attractive terms. The possibility of their becoming daily realities is remote because they are not talked about or considered in a way that gives them a real quality. To make a start in a new pattern of living would be like crossing a picket line or defying local religious customs and subjecting oneself to the ridicule of being a religious beatnik. In a small group that professes a dedication to the Christian life these subjects can be explored. Within the group, members may find that they are suffering from the same inhibitions and may be willing to make a change if they feel that others will give them acceptance and support. Others who had never considered such practices as a path to holiness might investigate them more fully and become attracted by their possibilities. The very involvement in a discussion of them can bring this kind of response. A group that is honest with itself has a creativeness which is distinct from the creativeness of each individual and is greater than the sum of the creativity of the individuals. Out of the members' searching and halting efforts at dealing with reality in the presence of each other come friendships which give moorings to lives.

We must not conclude that every Catholic lay group, even those organized into smaller units, produces these effects. A sampling of opinions of members of typical lay organizations by Dr. John J. O'Connor (in the April, 1962, issue of *The Lamp*) led him to this conclusion: "The most common criticism was that the vast majority of lay organizations haven't the slightest interest or intention of accomplishing anything. They are primarily social clubs, composed of like-minded friends who enjoy a good lecture, good conversation and good coffee every week or every month in a comfortably furnished home. Such meetings are less expensive than bowling, less tiresome than television, more stimulating than reading a book. This is good clean fun. How they are in any way related to 'restoring all things in Christ' is not immediately apparent." Since such groups avoid an encounter with Christianity, they will not likely provoke an encounter for their members with themselves or with each other.

Most lay people have never read the entire Bible. Many plan to read it at some time, but few ever achieve that goal. Great Books clubs have been organized precisely on this psychological fact. Few people will ever read the classics unless they form into groups which commit them to follow a planned course of reading. When they feel inclined to put off the assigned reading until they have more leisure or more favorable conditions, they remember their responsibility to the group and suffer the inconvenience entailed in doing the reading now. There will always be the exceptional person who seems to thrive on being estranged from the crowd. But the vast majority of people will or will not read the classics of the spiritual life or contemporary Christian thought depending upon the presence or absence of group motivation.

When lay people in groups dig into the reality of some present social condition, they are inclined to do whatever background reading is necessary. When one member comments on something significant which he has read, he is implicitly encouraging the others to read the same piece of literature or to extend his interest by reading on some other phase of the problem. When people are discussing articles which they have read or books which they are reading, they are encouraging and supporting spiritual reading and Catholic contemporary thought as an integrated part of the Christian life in a more effective way than the reading list, the book club, or pulpit exhortation.

The Christian is a human being who, like others, develops through his associations with others. He needs a community for growth as a fish needs water. Just as the hermits of the desert gave way to the modern form of monastic or religious community life, so must the isolated lay Catholic give way to the lay Christian who finds a new freedom as a Catholic through participation in a small group of like-minded people. The emergence of the small-group community contrasts with the previous emphasis of the Church in developing lay Catholics as isolated individuals. The new found Catholic community described in this chapter more closely resembles the Christian communities of the first three centuries than the large-membership organizations of past decades.

The strength of the Church in the future will lie less in its huge institutions and its bureaucratic processes, and more in its small groups of Christocentric apostolic lay Catholics. The small group can offer to its members something of the support religious life assures its members. Ideally religious life offers its members a path to Christian perfection. It gives them a rule of life, religious practices designed to inculcate the Christian spirit, and community support for the common quest for union with God.

Popes, bishops, priests, through encyclicals, pastorals, speeches, writings are calling lay people to the apostolate. Their call will have little meaning until we have friends to remind us, shame us by example, urge us, and call upon us for assistance. This will happen when we become a member of a band of people who are, as a group, on fire with zeal for the Kingdom. As time goes on we may need less urging and become more self-propelled. The real danger is to think that we can continue indefinitely without the support and encouragement of fellow sharers in the work of fulfilling the Christian vocation. Even the zealous missionary needs the companionship of fellow apostles, if he is not to turn into a self-anointed martyr who lives as a hardened and defensive foreigner in the land to which he has been sent.

The Sodality, Confraternity of Christian Doctrine discussion groups, Cana, Christian Family Movement, Young Christian Workers, Young Christian Students, Grail, the Legion of Mary, the St. Vincent de Paul Society, the training sessions and local units of the National Council of Catholic Men and the National Council of Catholic Women, and other small-group organizations in the Church which for their primary units have small face-to-face groups and which continue their associations outside of meetings, offer great possibilities for the Catholic layman. Through them he can acquire, strengthen, and find support for his Catholic values which may not be upheld in his neighborhood and places of work and recreation. The larger Church groups which have lengthy business meetings and financial reports, speeches and letter-writing campaigns, are not able to offer the support which the small, intimate group offers.

If the members of such groups are honest with themselves and each other and attempt to carry into their lives the implications of their discussions, their meetings can be raised to the level of religious experiences. Like the disciples at Emmaus as they talked over the passion and death of their Master "with the stranger," they will occasionally experience the presence of Christ. Members, looking back at meetings in which they confronted the vital message of Christ, will say to each other: "Were not our hearts burning within us as He was speaking?" Their experience will be a fulfillment of the promise that "where two or three are gathered together in My name, there I am in the midst of them."

XVI

SPIRITUAL COUNSEL

When we read the lives of the saints, we are often impressed with the attribution of the spiritual growth of the saint to the skillful guidance of a spiritual director. With childish simplicity, we might imagine that the only reason we have not achieved greater heights of sanctity is that we have not yet met the confessor or spiritual counselor who is tailored to our specifications. We may be searching for one who will clear a path for us by telling us clearly what he thinks we should do in the confusing and contradictory situations which we feel are entrapping us and keeping us from scaling the peaks of sanctity.

This image of the necessity of a spiritual father-figure becomes more deeply imbedded when we see it listed as an admonition in the Sodality handbook for lay people: "As far as possible, each member should select a devout, learned, and prudent priest as his fixed confessor. Without reserve, he shall manifest his conscience to his confessor and be formed and directed by him in all that pertains to the spiritual life." This statement taken at face value raises many questions. Do I really need a spiritual guide? Must a spiritual guide be a priest? Could I have more than one guide? How do I go about the process of determining which confessors are "devout, learned and prudent"? Can I permit *anyone* to direct me in the area of my life where I should cherish freedom most, in my relations with God and my fellow men?

Before we can answer these questions, we must deal with some semantic problems. Spiritual direction has long been an accepted term in the literature of spirituality. Today, however, the term has taken on a dictatorial connotation. It seems opposed to our modern emphasis on spiritual maturity and our call to "the freedom of the glory of the sons of God." For this reason, I prefer to use the expression "spiritual counsel." Counseling is based upon the belief that the person alone is capable of, and must ultimately accept responsibility for, his own decisions. Spiritual growth or maturity depends upon an ability and willingness to accept responsibility for oneself.

Lay people increasingly are complaining about the priest's failure to give them spiritual counsel through the sacrament of Penance. The layman can be unrealistic in his expectations in regard to this sacrament. The priest deserves a hearing. The primary responsibility of the priest is to determine the suitability of the person for the reception of the sacrament and to actually confer it. With routine confessions he may presume the necessary dispositions and simply give a penance and absolution. With people who confess a habit of serious sin, he may make inquiry into the penitent's serious purpose of amendment. This is the basic minimum which the priest does when he is deluged with unending lines of penitents or is himself indisposed.

Some priests, going beyond the call of duty, offer advice on the virtues opposed to the vices confessed. Of necessity this advice must be generalized. Unless the penitent is a regular client, pointed remarks, like stabs in the dark, may miss the mark and be damaging. In such a brief encounter it is almost impossible to assess the moral capabilities and real needs of the person. It is simply the difficulty of two strangers with different frames of reference and different vocabularies and motivations trying to communicate.

Many people who have no particular desire to establish a

regular program of spiritual counsel through the sacrament of Penance do make the practice of going to the same priest regularly to confess their customary lapses and imperfections. This becomes a source of security to the Catholic. When a perplexing spiritual crisis occurs, he knows that the confessor will be a source of reassurance. The confessor will feel less hesitant to make an affirmative statement and the penitent will have the confidence of dealing with someone whose judgment has been proved.

It is presumed that every priest wants to help his penitents to scale the heights of sanctity by helping them form Christian consciences. However he does not ordinarily set himself up as the sole anointed messenger of God. Experience has proved to him that many people, both among the frequent and infrequent penitents, do not wish to be disturbed by a priest who challenges them. They may go through life examining their conscience at a grade-school level of morality and find that confession is both comforting and comfortable. It poses no threat to their established way of life. What they want from the priest is for him to listen with understanding, offer a consoling or encouraging word, and give them absolution. The opening of new paths to sanctity or new categories for their examination of conscience is too disturbing.

In spite of a tradition that does not expect lay people to do much more than avoid mortal sin, there is an emerging segment of the laity who have been awakened by the call of Catholic Action and the Holy Spirit and who are seeking a deeper spiritual underpinning for their daily encounter with the world. Indeed they see the confessor as a God-anointed "savior" delivering them by absolution from Satan's bondage; they also see him as a Moses who can lead them through the meshes and mire of their earthly encounter to the heavenly Jerusalem. The fact that the confessor himself is afflicted with human weakness becomes an asset. In St. Paul's words, "He is able to have compassion on the ignorant and erring, because he himself also is beset with weakness...." Lay people are increasingly probing for better relationships with priests as spiritual guides or counselors both in and out of confession.

The selection of a confessor can be a formidable task. How does one find a priest who can do more than absolve one? Ideal priests do not exist. Everyone must settle for the only kind that do exist—real ones. Church law permits freedom to the laity in finding this kind of help. A wife reports about her quest: "I have searched out a confessor whose counsel is spendid; it took six years of inquiry, on and off, to find him."

The parish, simply on the basis of convenience, should not be overlooked. A housewife offers this practical bit of advice to people who do find a counselor or confessor after much search but then see him leave the city: "I seek spiritual counsel from the pastor of our parish since pastors in our diocese are less likely to be transferred than assistants." On the contrary, a business executive finds pastors less desirable, for a different reason: "I find that for me, the priest-counselor must be actively engaged in the apostolate to have some feel for my problems and aspirations. I find this only in assistants. They are regularly moved in this diocese to impossible distances. I have had four in the past three years. Presently I am without one."

A few tips on seeking help might be in order. If an unidentified woman asks a priest in confession to be her spiritual director, he may be reluctant to accept the request. He is apt to think of all the works on mysticism he has not read and of his personal limitations in living a deep spiritual life. If the same woman merely said, "Father, I am continually nagging my husband. Could you help me?" she might get a hearing and gradually the area of assistance could be extended to all of life. The priest who is intimidated about leading people to the heights of sanctity when confronted with human situations which are spiritual problems may prove to be another Curé d'Ars. After a trial period the person could begin to identify himself in order to help the priest relate in some way the present confession with past ones.

If lay people do not make too much out of their spiritual problems and simply present their difficulties in a human way to the priest, he can help them to interpret these spiritual difficulties in terms of human nature, the Cross, the sacramental and nonsacramental aids to increasing the divine life. This places the burden for initiating and sustaining the dialogue on the penitent. In any kind of a fruitful counseling relationship attention must be centered on felt needs. This is not a classroom procedure. It is the method parents use in training and teaching children. The immediate, apparent need is the starting point. Since the spiritual life is all of a piece, every difficulty in the spiritual life can be ultimately related to all the other aspects of it.

Priestly counsel need not be confined to the confessional. It is often done more effectively in the rectory. This poses many practical difficulties. The number of people any priest can see in the course of a month cannot be great. Then there is the occasional difficulty of getting past an unfriendly housekeeper. There is the chore of scheduling appointments for the priest, who ordinarily does not order his day in the manner of a doctor or social worker.

Most Catholics are aware that they can make appointments with any of the parish priests to deal with crises, such as a failing marriage, but there are few who come to the rectory without any serious vice or personal crisis and ask for help in becoming holy. This is still an uncommon enough phenomenon to create uncomfortable moments for many priests.

The following statements are curbstone views of laymen on the subject. A father of a family writes from experience: "I seek spiritual counsel regularly through a priest outside the parish by going to confession to him once a month. Seeking help in the confessional rather than outside is primarily a matter of convenience since I can find time with this particular priest whom I find helpful in hearing confessions. I believe it might be more helpful if spiritual guidance were available in a more informal setting than in the confessional, when I could talk with the priest at greater length. At one time when my wife and I were able to receive such spiritual counsel together, I found it more helpful."

Is there any way of categorizing the areas of spiritual counsel in a priest-lay relationship? A few people have indicated their expectations: "Inspiration is the kind of help we like from a priest." "The kind of help I would like from a priest is encouragement, advice on how to carry on in my vocation, a deeper insight into spirituality and how it applies to me personally; also how to bring Christ to others." "The help I get from a priest is an ever-growing knowledge of God in order to love and serve Him and myself. . . . He helps me to know myself which without help I never could. He suggests ways to correct my faults." Another includes the following areas for assistance: "Prayer, important decisions, spiritual problems, such as poverty and the virtues."

A woman states her needs in terms of receiving advice: "I want advice on how to become more Christlike and how to do this through the Mass, sacraments, reading, prayer, penance, growth in virtue and so forth. Occasionally I want help with a specific problem." The next is from a man who is more interested in talking than listening to advice: "I prefer the kind of person who will give me time to talk out a problem rather than offering too much advice."

Is there a point of spiritual maturity when a person has no need for further spiritual counsel? It seems to me that this sentence from Abbot Marmion is an oversimplification: "The purpose of direction is to help the soul do without direction." The question seems more delicately refined by the middle-aged mother of a family: "I'm not sure I am maturing spiritually; the constant ebb and flow frequently throws one. Many authors suggest one should become independent in one's spiritual life, but I should think mature guidance would always prove helpful. Every stage brings its own problems."

A husband speaking for himself and his spouse expresses their need for continued spiritual counsel in terms of advancement in the spiritual life: "We do not seek spiritual counsel very often. When some outstanding problem presents itself, our pastor or an assistant is the one usually consulted, sometimes in confession, sometimes outside. We find ourselves going to confession less now than before we were married, probably because serious sin is rarely a part of our lives. We find more need for guidance in advancement in the spiritual life, not less, because the more we become acquainted with higher degrees of perfection, the more unhappy we are with our present state. We do not seek nearly enough help in this area."

Undoubtedly what Abbot Marmion and others are warning against is overdependence on the spiritual counselor. Any counseling relationship can go askew and confirm a person in his immaturity and overdependence. The priest can identify himself with the penitent or client to the point that he assumes responsibility for figuring out solutions and even participating in their implementation. The priest must be able to objectify his own emotions and not fall into the trap of overidentification. He must continually remind the overdependent person that the problem at hand is not the counselor's. As a counselor he cannot assume responsibility for someone else's difficulty. He must be always a guide rather than a prop. A person can never mature as an individual until he can completely rely on his own resources for every eventuality in life. This delicate balance between the ability to be independent with a reasonable dependence upon others for counsel is the quintessence of maturity.

How long does one commit oneself to a counseling relationship? Does one outgrow a confessor or guide? A counseling relationship should last only as long as it is fruitful. There are plateaus in every relationship. Growth in human awareness is not plotted evenly on a graph but better described as moving from plateau to plateau. One can outgrow a counselor like he outgrows clothes. Briefly, the layman should seek out a spiritual counselor when he feels the need for counsel and pursue the relationship to the degree and for the length of time that it remains helpful.

CONCLUSION

PETER OF EAST ST. LOUIS

Since Our Blessed Lord has called all lay people to sanctity, the modern lay Christian would like to see a profile of the type of saint he is expected to be. In the language of Madison Avenue, what kind of an image should the twentieth-century layman project? Instead of a plan for sanctity which might be a lifeless and forbidding catalogue of virtues to be acquired and vices to be avoided, is there a way of constructing the model of a Christian who would be a fleshing out of these essays on sanctity for the layman? In the classical Church writings, Paul of Tarsus is the image of the militant apostolic Christian. He was known simply as *the* apostle. Is Paul's life so different from ours? Could he still be a model for the modern apostle?

The great figures of the Old and New Testaments had a vocation-experience, a sudden awareness or a growing realization that crystallized into the burning conviction that they had been called by God to perform a specific task for Him. With Paul of Tarsus the experience was dramatic, even traumatic:

I was on my way, approaching Damascus, when suddenly about noon there shone round about me a great light from heaven; and I fell to the ground and heard a voice saying to me, "Saul, Saul, why dost thou persecute Me?" And I answered,

"Who art thou, Lord?" And He said to me, "I am Jesus of Nazareth, Whom thou art persecuting." And my companions saw indeed the light, but they did not hear the voice of Him Who was speaking to me. And I said, "What shall I do, Lord?" And the Lord said to me, "Get up and go into Damascus, and there thou shalt be told of all that thou art destined to do." And as I could not see because of the dazzling light, my companions had to lead me by the hand, and so I reached Damascus. Now one Ananias . . . said to me, "Brother Saul, regain thy sight." And instantly I looked at him. And he said, "The God our Father has appointed thee beforehand to learn His will and to see the just One and to hear a voice from His mouth; for thou shalt be His witness before men of what thou hast seen and heard. And now why dost thou delay? Get up and be baptized and wash away thy sins, calling on His name."

Peter of East St. Louis, aged twenty-seven, has finished his schooling, is married with a wife and two children. He wears a gray flannel suit to work. At the urging of his wife, he has yielded and joined a parish group for couples. After a few months of having his values and cherished illusions questioned, he was struck by a sentence from a Gospel passage the group was discussing: "My meat is to do the will of Him Who sent me." For days afterwards he was quiet, reflective, peaceful. He was coming to grips for the first time in his adult life with the notion of Christian vocation. Unlike Paul of Tarsus, he was not blinded and prostrated, but he was undergoing a vocation-experience. Every desire in his life was held under the searching rays of God's personal love for him. The experience created anxieties and tensions in his life. He shared these with his wife. The message was clear. God was calling him to sanctity. In a sense everything was at stake as he saw dimly into the future: his nights out with the boys, the country club membership he looked forward to, a more expensive car, a more exclusive residential area, the quiet evenings of uninterrupted TV boredom, the switch from *Sports Illustrated* to the Bible. If he accepted the call, he would be haunted by the words of Paul of Tarsus, *You are not your own*. The decision of Peter of East St. Louis for Christ or comfort would depend largely on the support or lack of it from Alice, his wife. They would have to share and accept the vision together or live guilt-ridden lives.

Peter accepted his vocation. But a vocation which is accepted needs to ripen and develop into a complete commitment to Christ. Paul of Tarsus was obsessed with his identification with Christ. *With Christ I am nailed to the cross. It is now no longer I that live, but Christ lives in me. And the life that I now live in the flesh, I live in the faith of the Son of God, Who loved me and gave Himself up for me.*

Peter of East St. Louis saw a headline in a national Catholic weekly: "Today's Christian must find a new method of training for sanctity." It has a hollow ring to him. It sounds as though we only need discover a gimmick which will mass produce Christian witnesses. He knows that he must bear in himself a personal love for Christ and struggle each day to bring every thought, word, and action of his life under the gentle sway and enriching influence of the Christ-life. He knows that his fidelity to his commitment or decision for Christ will depend upon his prayer life. Presently there is no possibility of his going to Mass daily, so he must settle for Saturday and Sunday and make an act of spiritual communion wherein he expresses his ardent desire to be present with Christ sacramentally. Because of this desire to be present to offer himself with Christ at his parish altar, he is confident that Christ will give him the daily bread of actual graces *in absentia*.

To Paul of Tarsus Christ and His Church formed a unity through the Spirit. *For as the body is one and has many members, and all the members of the body, many as they are, form one body, so also is it with Christ. . . . If one member suffers anything, all the members suffer with it, or if one member glories, all the members rejoice with it. Now you are the body of Christ, member for member.*

Peter of East St. Louis has a love for Christ that finds its expression in the totality of his human relationships. Finding Christ at the Eucharistic table leads him to Christ in the market place, the highways, the office building, the neighborhood, his home. In the most sordid of human circumstances he learns to find, robed in the flesh which the Word inhabits, the Christ who sits at the right hand of His Father. Social and economic status, skin pigmentation, national origin, level of education, job classification cannot interfere with the I-Thou encounter he seeks with each person.

Peter is more concerned with organizations than Paul of Tarsus, who lived in a simpler society. There had been no explosions of population, technology, democracy, and communications in Paul's time. There was no need for big business, big unions, and big government. Peter of East St. Louis realizes that if his charity is to abound in his world, his passionate love for Christ's body must find its expression in and through our highly organized society. He understands charity in terms of meetings which are called to deal with common problems. He finds himself taking minutes, getting out a monthly bulletin, making the necessary phone calls between meetings, attending luncheon meetings, answering mail in an effort to do what Paul did by a speech, a conversation, or an epistle. Peter cannot visualize Paul of Tarsus operating any other way than he himself does in twentieth-century urban America.

Paul of Tarsus was no rocking-chair apostle. *When we came to Macedonia, our flesh had no rest; we had troubles on every side, conflicts without and anxieties within. . . . From the Jews five times I received forty lashes less one. Thrice I was scourged, once I was stoned, thrice I suffered shipwreck, a night and a day I was adrift on the sea; in journeyings often, in perils from floods, in perils from robbers, in perils from my own nation, in perils from the Gentiles, in perils in the city, in perils in the wilderness, in perils in the seas, in perils from false brethren; in labor and hardships, in many sleepless nights, in hunger and thirst, in fastings often, in cold and nakedness. Besides those outer things, there is my daily pressing anxiety, the care of all the churches.*

As the years go on Peter of East St. Louis becomes increasingly involved in the concerns of his work, his local government, his neighborhood, his parish church, the ecumenical movement. People impose upon his generosity. At times he feels betrayed by friends or more often he does not feel that they are pulling their weight. His golf suffers. His lawn is not as well trimmed as those on both sides of him. Repairs are not made as quickly as before. The family meals and his clothing are less expensive because of higher phone and gasoline bills. While Peter does not spend less time reading the paper, he reads with more compassion. The people of Africa and Asia are his blood brothers in Christ.

Paul of Tarsus could speak of his weakness as he did of his strength. *Who is weak and I am not weak. . . . If I must boast I will boast of the things that concern my weakness. . . . And lest the greatness of the revelations should puff me up, there was given me a thorn for the flesh, a messenger of Satan, to buffet me. Concerning this I thrice besought the Lord that it might leave me. And He has said to me, "My grace is sufficient for thee, for strength is made perfect in weakness." Gladly therefore I will glory in my infirmities, that the strength of Christ may dwell in me. Wherefore I am satisfied, for Christ's sake, with infirmities, with insults, with hardships, with persecutions, with distresses. For when I am weak, then I am strong.*

Peter of East St. Louis is cited by his employer for his professional competence, by the local community by being chosen chairman of the United Fund campaign, by his pastor for his willingness to be a lector at Mass each Sunday. Yet when Peter examines his conscience at the end of the day, he is aware of the feeling of depression he had when he came home from work, his lack of tenderness with his wife, and his failure to give attention to the interests of his children. He complained about the lethargy of his fellow workers on the fund drive. He asked himself why he had been foolish enough to accept so much responsibility. To his finger tips he feels the weight of his humanity. His day seems like a trail of neglected opportunities. The mystery of why God chose this vessel of clay to become His messenger in heralding the Good News by his way of life frightens him. Like Paul he finds consolation in the conviction that his strength lies in his weakness.

Although Paul said of himself "our flesh had no rest," he was speaking of a particular mood. He was not a compulsive activist ridden with guilt about enjoying a spare moment or a pleasurable experience. He learned to accept both the bitter and the sweet and thank God equally for each. *I know how to live humbly and I know how to live in abundance (I have been schooled to every place and every condition), to be filled and to be hungry, to have abundance and to suffer want. I can do all things in him who strengthens me.*

Peter of East St. Louis needs seasoning. He overextends himself because he has not learned to say "no." He easily becomes emotionally drained by listening to people's troubles. Alice, caught by her husband's new vigor for action, feels she must join everything she can possibly squeeze into her calendar. She, too, feels guilty about enjoying a novel or a movie. At times she even suffers guilt feelings about the time she gives to routine housework. It seems that Peter and Alice can only learn by their excesses to ride the tides and harmonize their own human needs with the needs of their family and the community. Harmony is the result of counsel, patience, and an adequate prayer life. As prayer deepens their insights and they come to a growing awareness of their true selves, they can share more of the world's anxieties without themselves becoming neurotic. Eventually they will learn to enjoy, without pangs of guilt, the simple life, the natural joys of family and social life.

Peace and joy are nebulous qualities. While Paul seems outwardly to be embroiled in conflict, inwardly he is at peace and his life has an all-pervasive serenity. He says to all the Peters who will walk in his path: *Rejoice in the Lord always; again I say rejoice. Let your moderation be known to all men. The Lord is near. Have no anxiety, but in every prayer and supplication with thanksgiving let your petitions be made known to God. And may the peace of God which surpasses all understanding guard your hearts and your minds in Christ Jesus.* Peace and joy will come eventually to Peter and be reflected in Alice if daily, with docility and humility, he is faithful to his vision. He must think of the acquiring of Christian maturity, not in terms of weeks or months, but of years and decades.

Although burdened with an awareness of his many weaknesses, Peter abounds in hope. He experiences the joy of combat as he carries the burden of his humanity. Peter does not have the depth of Paul, but he can sing in his heart the lyrical expression of Paul's indomitable love of Christ: *Who shall separate us from the love of Christ? Shall tribulation, or distress, or persecution, or hunger, or nakedness, or danger, or the sword? Even as it is written, "For thy sake we are put to death all the day long. We are regarded as sheep for the slaughter." But in all these things we overcome because of Him who has loved us. For I am sure that neither death, nor life, nor angels, nor principalities, nor things present, nor things to come, nor powers, nor height, nor depth, nor any other creature, will be able to separate us from the love of God, which is in Christ Jesus our Lord.*

The source of joy for Paul, the ardor of his hope and the depth of his love, was rooted in his faith in Christ's resurrection. If Peter listens with docility to the Spirit, he will learn the hidden meaning of Paul's admonition to him: *Therefore, if you have risen with Christ, seek the things that are above, where Christ is seated at the right hand of God. Mind the things that are above, not the things that are on earth. For you have died and your life is hidden with Christ in God. When Christ, your life, shall appear, then you too will appear with Him in Glory.*